LIVING ON YOUR OWN

LIVING

ON YOUR OWN

Single Women, Rental Housing,
and Post-Revolutionary Affect
in Contemporary South Korea

JESOOK SONG

Cover art: "Colored (Eye) Glasses (*saek-an-gyŏng*)" by Seung won Oh. Used by permission.

Poem, chapter 4: "For Suk" by Ch'oe Sŭng-ja via Munhak kwa chisŏngsa. Used by permission.

Photograph, chapter 4: "Young Demonstrators at Candlelight Vigil in 2008" by Seung hwa Park. Used by permission.

Published by
STATE UNIVERSITY OF NEW YORK PRESS
Albany

© 2014 State University of New York

For information, contact
State University of New York Press
www.sunypress.edu

Production, Laurie Searl
Marketing, Anne M. Valentine

Library of Congress Cataloging-in-Publication Data

Song, Jesook
    Living on your own : single women, rental housing, and post-
revolutionary affect in contemporary South Korea / Jesook Song.
        pages cm
    Includes bibliographical references and index.
    ISBN 978-1-4384-5013-1 (hc : alk. paper) 978-1-4384-5012-4 (pb : alk. paper)
    1. Single women—Housing—Korea (South) 2. Rental housing—Korea
(South) 3. Single women—Korea (South) I. Title.
    HQ1765.5.S654 2014
    306.81'53095195—dc23   2013012832

10   9   8   7   6   5   4   3   2   1

dedicated to

the late Choi Myung-Sook

Contents

Acknowledgments

I would like to thank first and foremost the single women who allowed me to intimately learn about their journeys. I particularly want to thank the sixteen women whose narratives and lives are introduced in this book. Although their names are pseudonyms, I list them here as a sign of my deep appreciation: Chagyông, Chisu, Chunhee, Haein, Hosôn, Kyuri, Minsô, Miyông, Nani, Pohûi, Sojông, Sônu, Tojin, Togyông, Wony, and Yoon. I changed all pseudonyms as first names in this book although I used last names for the same people in previous publications. I admire them for being so strong, genuine, and grounded despite the ruptures they have experienced between their social consciousness and their individual happiness, between their ideal of autonomy and the realities of financial and moral pressures, and between their loss of social networks and their hope to create new kinds of social support. It is their trust in me—their willingness to tell stories that are not always easy to share—that honors me the most.

I am indebted to the many people who kindly offered their time and input as well as to the institutions that provided generous financial support. The field research for this book was funded by the Korea Research Foundation (KRF 05-R-28), the Academy of Korean Studies (AKS-2006-R-48), and the Connaught New Staff Matching Grant at the University of Toronto (2005–2007). The initial stage of writing the book was funded by the Korea Foundation (2008–2009).

I am grateful to have had the opportunity to develop my ideas in workshops, conferences, and lectures in diverse disciplines, including Korean studies, Asian studies, anthropology, ethnographic studies, sociology, urban studies, and women and gender studies. At the University of Toronto, these opportunities included the Socio-Cultural and Linguistic Anthropology Workshop in the Department of Anthropology (2009), Markets and Modernities in Asia at the Asian Institute (2009), the Senior Common Room Lecture at University College (2009), the Workshop on Challenges, Dynamics and Implications of Welfare Regime Change in Comparative Perspective (2009), the Research Seminar at the Women and Gender Studies Institute (2010), and the Feminism and the Politics of Appropriation Conference (2011). I also presented my work at the Korean Studies Workshop at the University of Illinois at Urbana-Champaign (2006); the American Ethnological Society Annual Spring Meeting (2007); the American Anthropological Associations Annual Meetings (2007, 2009, 2010); the Korean Studies Workshop at the University of British Columbia (2008); the Canadian Anthropological Association Annual Meeting (2009); the workshops Gender and Politics in Contemporary Korea, at the University of British Columbia (2009), and Affect and Markets in East Asia, at Simon Fraser University (2009); the Urban and Regional Development Panel at the International Sociological Association (2010); the Colloquium of the Gender Research Institute, Yonsei University, Seoul, South Korea (2011); the Speakers' Series in the Center for Asian and Pacific Studies, at the University of Iowa (2012); the Colloquium Series on Korean Cultural Studies, at Columbia University (2013); the Korean Studies Speakers' Series in the East Asian Program and the Colloquium of the Department of Anthropology at Cornell University (2013); and the lecture series in the East Asia Center at the University of Virginia (2014). I am also fortunate to have had informal settings for discussion, such as an affect reading group, a weekly writing group, and my graduate course, The Anthropology of Neoliberalism.

Although significantly changed in this book, earlier versions of some of the content appear in "'A Room of One's Own': The Meaning of Spatial Autonomy for Unmarried Women in Neoliberal South Korea" (Song 2010) and "Between Flexible Life and Flexible Labor: The Inadvertent Convergence of Socialism and Neoliberalism in South Korea" (Song 2009a). The latter article received a Distinguished Paper Award from the Academy of Korean Studies in 2010. I thank for the permissions of using the poem, "For Suk," from Ch'oe Sûng-ja, the photo of Candlelight Vigil in 2008 from Seung hwa Park, and the painting, "Colored (Eye) Glasses (saek-an-gyông)," for cover design from Seung won Oh

A number of people offered substantial comments and direct assistance in the rich process of writing this book: Nancy Abelmann, Greg Albo, Kristina Alda, Ann Anagnost, Ruoyun Bai, Jiwon Bang, Joshua Barker, Li Chen, Mun Young Cho, Yeoul Cho-Yi, Hyaeweol Choi, Hae Yeon Choo, Jennifer Jihye Chun, Francis Cody, Girish Daswani, Naisargi Dave, Maureen

FitzGerald, Caren Freeman, Andrew Gilbert, Salvatore Giusto, Laam Hae, Judy Ju Hui Han, Matt Hilder, Theodore Hughes, David Hulchanski, Im-Na Yoon Kyung, Kajri Jain, Jin Yoo-Mi, Seung Hwa Joung, Jung Hye-shin, Jiyeon Kang, Soo Dol Kang, the late William Francis Kelleher Jr., Kim Dong-Choon, Hana Kim, Hyun Mee Kim, Kyung-Hee Kim, Kyoung-yim Kim, Laura Kim, Seung-Kyung Kim, Sungjo Kim, Susie Kim, Chris Krupa, Huikian Kwee, Jinhwa Lee, Kang-Kook Lee, Namhee Lee, Yoonhee Lee, Tania M. Li, Victor Li, Yanfei Li, Bonnie McElhinny, David McNally, Kris Meen, Hirokazu Miyazaki, Seungsook Moon, Andrea Muehlehbach, Sanjukta Mukherjee, Beverley Mullings, Michelle Murphy, Valentina Napolitano, Laura Nelson, Stephen Nugent, Seo Young Park, Pak Su-jin, Misun Park, Katharine Rankin, Sonia Ryang, Shiho Satsuka, Dong Jin Seo, Hyun Bang Shin, Kwang-Yeong Shin, Rachel Silvey, Allan Smart, Gavin Smith, Alissa Trotz, Toshiko Tsujimoto, Melinda Vandenbeldgiles, Jeremy Withers, Joseph Wong, Jie Yang, Sunyoung Yang, Joshua Young, as well as anonymous readers. I particularly thank Jane Springer, a professional editor and a good friend who helped make my writing clearer and more accessible.

I would like to thank Nancy Ellegate, acquisitions editor, and Laurie Searl, production editor, and their co-workers at SUNY Press, including Michael Rinella, Catherine Chilton, Jen Stelling, and Anne Valentine, for patiently and kindly advising me through the book production process.

Thanks to dear friends and families in Toronto and elsewhere: Aldyth's family, Ari and Dori's family, David's family, Isa's family, Kai's family, Maru and Namu's family, Nari's family, Eunice, Eunjung, Hyejung, Jamie, Julie, Laam, Marsha, So Jin, and Soo-Jung, and Yoonjung. And my deepest thanks and love to Hon-Yee and Kara.

Introduction

* ◈ •————————• ◈ *

Single Women, Rental Housing, and Post-Revolutionary Affect in the Context of the Global Youth Crisis

You know, the government is now encouraging births, saying it's serious that Korea has entered a stage of an aging population and a decreasing number of workers. Women's organizations are asking who's going to take care of children when women don't have support for child care from government. If anyone raises the issue of single women's (*pihon yôsông*) needs in this context, they wouldn't take it seriously, no way (*ssi to an môkil kôt kat ta*).[1]

—Hosôn

During my doctoral research on the impact of neoliberalism in South Korea, on the brink of the Asian Financial Crisis in the late 1990s, I met many frustrated, young, unmarried women who had just graduated from college and university. They had few opportunities to enter the job market. Part of the younger generation called the "new poor," they were affected by the collapsing national economy and the resurgent conservative gender regime that endorsed gender discrimination in the job market. Most of the young, unmarried women I interviewed were working in a range of irregular jobs, such as in temporary public works programs at minimum wage; in rank-and-file, grassroots organizations for less than minimum wage; or as tutors in the private education market, with no job security. During the late 1990s, South Korean young people's severe unemployment and heightened frustration appeared to be unusual both in Korea and globally.[2] However, with the strong youth participation in the spreading unrest following the 2008 global

I

financial crisis, it is easier to understand the challenging situation that faced Korean young adults a decade earlier.[3]

Both the Asian financial crisis in South Korea in the late 1990s and the 2008 global financial crisis have had severe impacts on local economies, in some cases resulting in governments' bankruptcy but in most cases spurring an unprecedentedly high rate of youth unemployment and a rapid rise in the cost of public goods and services, such as tuition at public universities. The Organisation for Economic Cooperation and Development (OECD) announced somewhat belatedly that it anticipates a long-term adverse effect on youth employment (Morison 2012), given the series of events following the 2008 global financial crisis demonstrating the intolerable situation of youth unemployment, including the Arab Spring in Africa and the Middle East, the crisis of the euro and political struggles in Europe since 2010, and the Québec student protests in Canada in 2012.[4] The globally spreading situation of youth unemployment is seamlessly connected to the situation of basic subsistence, including housing. This book presents young single women's experience of finding housing in South Korea as a window for viewing and for understanding the frustration and struggles of youth worldwide, with a focus on gendered and affective domains.[5]

Over and over, the young single women whose voices are at the heart of this book expressed their need for a place to live on their own as independent adults. They felt suffocated and invaded by their parents' supervision of their lives—from regulations about such things as staying at a friend's overnight or coming home late to heightened marriage pressure. On the one hand, it is hard for any young adult in South Korea, regardless of gender, to afford to buy or even rent his or her own place. That is because in Korea, a significant lump sum is required as a rental deposit. However, young men do not face the same parental supervision and regulation of sexuality that traditionally keep young women living at their parents' places until they marry (Kendall 1996, 2002). This gendered expectation comes from a belief that unmarried men's sexuality is a sign of virility, whereas unmarried women's sexuality is suppressed and readily associated with promiscuity (S-H. Lee 2002).[6] Further, the economic conditions for young single men are more favorable than for young single women: men have higher wage and promotional opportunities, and bank loans and credit are available for high-income earners, who are more likely to be men. This clear gender bias, in conjunction with the privileged status of marriage and the normative family, makes the lives of young women who want to live on their own particularly difficult. This kind of marginalization from kinship and gendered socioeconomic status is comparable to that faced by other subpopulations in South Korea that do not belong to normative adult life in society, such as queer populations and divorced women.

Rental housing is at the crux of financial class divisions in South Korea—between those who have money capital and those who do not. Rental housing is investigated in this book because it is the primary form of dwelling for working-class households, including unemployed or underemployed young single adults. This is true of rental housing in many countries. In Korea, rental housing provides a unique opportunity to think about the significance of the informal financial market and gift economy (family, friends, and private loans)—the way the working class maneuvers through the gap between wages and subsistence without relying on the formal financial market (bank loans). Korea's particular form of rental housing contributes to the polarization of financial classes and also regulates women's mobility and residential autonomy.

The relation between housing and financial markets is clearly exemplified through the case of the 2008 global financial crisis, which originated with the collapse of the U.S. subprime mortgage market thanks to reckless Wall Street financiers.[7] However, the mortgage market and its influence on the formal financial sector is presumed to be about the ownership of housing, and thus tenants are not so easily associated with housing finance as they are in the Korean case.[8] Further, formal financial institutions (banks and insurance companies) are the primary channel of housing loans in the United States, whereas in Korea, informal financial institutions, such as rotating credit associations and informal loans, have filled the gap to supply loans for low-income people.[9] Building on research on the significance of the informal sector to global capitalism, this book demonstrates how in South Korea financial products and practices became crucial to households' subsistence economy. By outlining the informal financialization (or sedimented financialization) that existed prior to the crisis and the formal financialization that began after the crisis (specifically, global financialization), this book shows the effects of the combined and converging systems on people's lives, using the case of Korean single women. An eye-opening implication of these young single women's difficulty in achieving residential autonomy is the prevalence of informal financial practices and their influence on the lives of the working poor. Lived experiences of these combined systems are demonstrated in chapters 1 and 2.

This book also depicts the unsettling affects that accompanied research participants in their efforts to survive and thrive in the post-revolutionary moment that arrived with neoliberal regimes from the late 1990s to the new millennium. In short, revolution here refers to radical social change by subaltern movement, and affect refers to the rapid and intense emotion that has an impact on people even before they are cognitively aware of it. Ninety percent of my research participants were student activists in the anti–military state movements. They also shared the experience of the end of the military regime and achievement of democratic polity throughout the early 1990s.[10] As a critical self-reflection of their male-dominated student activist organizations (that mirrored the male-centered and dogmatic hierarchy of the military state dictatorship), many of my research participants became involved in women's movements and nongovernmental organizations (NGOs, under the rubric of the civil society movement), which were less rigid and more open to marginal positions and identities than the student organizations. They became more critical of dogmatic political activism, identifying themselves in their position as women along with other marginalized identities. Although they loathed the capitalist appropriation of "needs" for leisure and self-development through consumerism, they were also won over by the liberal market ideology of enjoyment and persuaded to improve their personal lives, adapting the current "technologies of the self" of neoliberal capitalism in order to make life manageable in regard to pressure and desire seeking. Originating with Michel Foucault (1988), the concept of "technologies of the self" refers to the ways in which people constitute their own identities in the (western) philosophic tradition of the relationship between self-knowledge ("know yourself") and the practice of taking care of oneself ("attend yourself").[11] The fact that enjoyability became an imperative goal is understandable, considering that they had witnessed the suffering of student activists who had forsaken individual happiness for the political cause. Many of their fellow student activists died of physical injuries and posttraumatic stress resulting from state violence.[12] My research participants wanted to be socially conscious, but they also wanted to enjoy their lives—they wanted neither to be die-hard activists nor anonymous cubical office workers.

Thus, this book delves into the narratives of their experiences as former rank-and-file activists. Although their aspirations for social change and self-liberation helped produce democratization and social change, their contribution to history is invisible (M. Park 2005, N. Lee 2005). Further, their humble experiences *after* the revolution have received little attention from researchers. The recent student movement seems to have lost the militancy of the earlier student activism of which my research participants were a part, despite the fact that young adults' employment and living security in the neoliberal situation is not better than the predemocratization era.[13] The Korean post-revolution period, not unlike other places and times in world history, reveals that the cutting-edge activist spirit appears to succumb to inertia following post-revolutionary political concessions. This is accompanied by heightened individual consumerism and insufficient collective force to maintain a social base that could overturn the liberal market system.

However, the young single women with backgrounds as political activists are passionately seeking new ethics and praxis in the post-revolutionary era via a form of self-suspension—or "small vacations from the will," as Berlant (2007b) put it—and with their critical reflections on the revolutionary era and affect.[14] The book interprets my research participants' ongoing political and social activism as a form of self-suspension by drawing out salient affects of both the revolutionary and post-revolutionary eras (social duty and enjoyment, respectively). People who carry the memory of direct experience in the revolutionary movement and who at the same time acquired socially liberal attitudes in the course of the revolution have a unique potential to mobilize social change. Their personal and collective experiences provide useful insights for analyzing the current uprising of global youth, particularly about what to expect and prepare for *after* a revolution.

Situating the Single Women in This Book

I conducted research on thirty-five single women in their late twenties to late thirties, living apart from their parents and recruited through women's organizations and networks in metropolitan Seoul and Busan (South Korea's second-largest metropolitan area) in 2005–2007. Although I did not intend to solicit former student activists, the fact that 90 percent of recruited women identified themselves as such indicates their particular generational background. Regardless of marital status, it is the age group that experienced the unique historical moment of their country moving from a fascist state to a democracy with liberal governments. If I had begun my research half a decade later (that is, after 2012), recruiting single women in their thirties living apart from their parents, exposure to a draconian state and personal experience participating in the collective opposition to it would not have been a common feature. My research participants, who identify themselves as not bound for the marriage market (*pihon yŏsŏng*), are clearly aligned with feminist ideas of self-determination and women's autonomy as a result of their participation in the significant sociopolitical transformation toward democratization and liberalization.

Regardless of this particular generational characteristic, the number of single women in South Korea living on their own (mostly in rental housing) is growing. According to the 2006 report by the Korean National Statistical Office (KNSO), which conducts a census (*ch'ong in'gu chosa*) every five years, the number of single women's households (of women between the ages of 25 and 39) in 2000 was 200,915. They constituted only 3 percent of the population of women of the same age. In 2005, the number of single women's households in the same age group increased to 386,430, or 6.5

percent of the population of the same age. There was an increase of 92.3 percent in single women's households over the five years, in spite of the fact that the total population of women in that age group decreased by 7 percent during the same period. This corresponds, although not directly, to the increase of 42.5 percent in single-person households across gender and age between 2000 and 2005. Among women aged 24 to 39, never-married women increased by 12.4 percent and divorced women by 0.4 percent, and the number of married women went down by 12.7 percent between 2000 and 2005 (National Statistics Office 2006).

KNSO only began to include lone-living women's households in the national statistics in 2000, and KNSO cannot determine from the data it has from that period whether these were unmarried women or whether they owned or rented their homes (Yi Chi-ûn and Kang Ûn-jin, KNSO agents, pers. comm., December 13, 2005). This changed during the 2005 census, when KNSO began to collect data by type of residence (owned or rented) and marital status (unmarried, married, divorced, or widowed). In 2005, the census data show that 282,929 unmarried women (aged 25 to 39) lived in rented housing (88 percent); 8,080 in public housing (less than 3 percent); and 29,451 (9 percent) owned their houses or condos.[15] Although we cannot discern from these data whether the unmarried women were interested in marriage (*mihon*, meaning "not yet married") or not interested in marriage (*pihon*, meaning "unassociated with marriage")—*pihon* women are the focus of my research—it is clear that there has been a fast-growing population of unmarried women over the last decade.

This growth is reflected in the dramatic increase in the media representation of single women over the last decade. However, the typical media representation of young single women who live separately from their parents as upper-class family members or as successful professional women affluent enough to own their own housing (not renting) does not correspond to my informants' experience. Although the young single women in this research have educational capital, their economic standing falls into the new poor of the neoliberal economy. Both nationally and globally, studies show that well-educated youth who in the past would have become part of the regular workforce are now more likely to be precariously employed or remain unemployed (U and Pak 2007; U 2009).[16] All of the women in my study were college or university graduates, mostly from underprivileged schools that do not generate job prospects in big, well-established companies. Few of the women had stable and sustainable full-time employment. Most had part-time jobs or insecure subcontract jobs as tutors, after-school teachers, or entry-level independent salespersons. Similar to other metropolitan, underemployed young adults worldwide, these women are part of the era in which service, information, and knowledge industries that use the Internet have prevailed over the manufacturing industry's use of personal sales representatives. As Paolo Virno (2004) and Maurizio Lazzarato (1996) note, "immaterial labor," exemplified in service, communication, and human relations, became much more prevalent in post-Fordist production.[17] Further, as Hester Eisenstein (2009) points out—building on other feminist scholars, such as Bumiller (2008), Zillah Eisenstein (2007), Spivak (1999), and Stacy (1987)—although feminism has become popular in politics and in the media, gender equality has been compromised by corporate neoliberal capitalism, which appropriates feminism to stratify and make the workforce more elastic for the benefit of employers.

The only different or more accentuated aspect of these Korean single women's labor compared with Korean single men's labor is that the majority of the women never had periods of stable employment that compensated their educational capital, even during the manufacturing industry's most vital era. The feminization of precarious job markets in the heyday of industrial capitalism is a phenomenon that has been in place since the Korean War (1950–1953), if not before.[18] Young women who were mostly junior or high school graduates were the primary workforce for the national economy in the textile/garment/shoe factories of the 1970s. The exploitation of those young single women in light industrial manufacturing was predicated upon the cheap cost of their labor—they received low pay because manufactories assumed there would be quick turnover, as they expected that the women would work only until they got married. They were eventually kicked out of these manufacturing jobs by corporate owners who were refocusing on the automobile industry, according to the dictates of the military state's economic development planning (S. Chun 2003; H. M. Kim 2000; S-K. Kim 1997; Koo 2001; Song 2006b). However, even long after women were officially given equal access to higher education,[19] their participation in full-time employment was significantly lower than men's.[20] The feminization of the irregular job market worsened with the liberalization of the economy and of employment during and after the Asian financial crisis.

The inadequate employment of young single women with higher education exemplifies two tendencies in the labor market. First, part-time jobs have become the predominant form of employment through the neoliberalization of the labor market, in the name of restructuring; also, women occupy the majority of part-time jobs and men take up the reduced portion of full-time jobs. Second, since the crisis, young adults with a good education have rarely had the opportunity to enter the stable job market. Rather, they have become an industrial reserve army, or surplus population, "good-for-nothings" (paeksu), a label for the young adults who became the new poor in South Korea. This is not unique to Korea. Advanced capitalist societies have already experienced stagnation of employment in general and of university-educated people in particular. In East Asia, where most nations are known as successful, newly industrializing countries, the unemployment of well-educated young workers is a relatively new social phenomenon and predicament (for information about the situation in Japan, see Arai 2005, Slater 2003, Lukacs 2010a, 2010b; for Korea, U and Pak 2007, Song 2007, forthcoming; for China, Hoffman 2010, Zhang 2010).

For example, one of my research participants, Chunhee, an unmarried woman, was hired by a small company in the mid-1990s when she sought an office job after she graduated from university. She worked for five years at a monthly salary of around 1 million won (approximately $1,000), without being able to save much. Yoon, another single woman interviewee, said she worked in a small company with five employees until she left during the Asian financial crisis and quickly used up her savings while looking for a new job. Chunhee's and Yoon's experiences challenge the conventional image of women who graduate from university. The media often depicts young women graduates as having the impractical fantasy of working in well-paid office jobs in big companies and refusing to look for more humble jobs (nun'nopi rûl natuô ya). However, even when they have spent years working in a small company, because of the low salaries and poor benefits, most do not have enough savings to carry out their dreams of independent housing, an interesting career, or further study.

What is notable in the case of Korean young adults is housing constraints, particularly for unmarried women, despite the liberalized sociopolitical climate and the flourishing of loan products. On top of the fact that there is little or no credit for rental housing, what does exist is unavailable to people without a prestigious employment record. In addition, housing policies are discriminatory; they are based on the normative practices of marriage and the normative definition of family. Unmarried people less than thirty-five years old (without the experience of living by themselves for three years) do not qualify to apply for bank loans for the Korean rent system, called chônse, which requires a significant lump-sum deposit (see chapters 1 and 2). Although it affects both men and women who are not married, unmarried women are far more disadvantaged by the feminized and neoliberalizing job market, in which most available jobs for women are irregular or temporary work. Wony, one of my research participants, notes that "while it is not uncommon to see single men in their thirties get a loan, few single women in their thirties manage to get a loan because their annual income is less than the required 25 million won [approximately $25,000]." A friend of Wony's was able to receive a rental housing loan from a bank despite being under thirty-five because she married her common-law partner (her husband, because marriage in Korea does not include same-sex marriage).

Wony concludes that marriage is the only way to get a rental housing loan before a woman is thirty-five.

But unmarried women who want to live independently are not simply victims of the discriminatory housing system. All unmarried women who manage to live on their own against social convention clearly have strong, independent spirits. They are representative agents of women's resistance to patriarchal conventional norms, which demand that unmarried women live with their parents until they marry and that they get married at an "appropriate age." The perception of marriage as optional is increasing; some scholars even consider there to be a "significant shift from traditional conceptions of women's bodies as familial and societal property" (Jones 2006, 221). However, because of insecurity of employment and financing, marriage may be the only option for women who do not have a sufficient income or financial security.[21] In a context in which marriage is the time for the redistribution of familial and financial resources, these unmarried women show themselves to be quintessentially strong willed and self-determined. Many of my research participants were at the center of the women's movement, which had achieved, by 2005, the removal of the "family headship system" (hojuje) that had forced women to rely on male lineage for property rights, parental rights, and inheritance. For example, the family headship system problem is shown in the situation of homeless women (Song 2009b). Women leaving the family home with their children, even when escaping domestic violence, cannot enroll their children in schools because of the father's right to be informed of his children's location. Another example of the patriarchal family system being entrenched in government policy is the fact that women could not register themselves as candidates for entrepreneur incubator programs during the Asian financial crisis without patrilineal male kin members' sponsorship, even though the incubator programs were designed to ameliorate the dire situation of women-headed households. The nasty harassment by conservative social forces of women participants and activists in this movement for the removal of the family headship system (hojuje p'yeji undong) is akin to that experienced by North American prochoice activists, including physical confrontations, online stocking and hacking, and death threats.[22] Tojin, whose leftist and women's rights activism are presented in chapter 3, recalled in a trembling voice the memorable moment when she heard that the National Assembly had agreed to eliminate the family headship system. She said the new legislation was the most significant step forward in all her years of feminist activism and perhaps in Korean feminist history as a whole.

On another front, unmarried women have become vulnerable in a recently emerging social context. They have been the implicit target of national anxiety over the decreasing population and are under severe social pressure to marry and reproduce (as the opening quote from Hosôn's narrative reveals). Since the Asian financial crisis, South Korean society has been gravely concerned, if not panicked, by its low fertility rate (and aging society), which has led to various attempts to increase the reproduction of the national population. In 2005, the government announced a master plan (Republic of Korea 2005), called *Saeromaji pûl'laen* 2010 (New anticipation plan regarding low fertility and aging society) for the years 2006 to 2010.[23] Lamenting that South Korea has the world's lowest birth rate and its fastest-aging population, the plan asserts the need for a national focus on reproduction, centering on women in their twenties to mid-thirties. The late former president Roh Moo Hyun (2003–2008) pledged to provide tax breaks as well as help with child care and education expenses for households in which legally married women gave birth to a third child, a pledge that was never fulfilled.

Not unrelated are the changes South Korea is making in relation to the foreign migrant population in the name of "multiculturalism." Among the flow of many non-Korean nationals into South Korea are foreign brides, mostly from China and Southeast Asia, who have been allowed to immigrate on the condition that they marry Korean peasant or urban poor bachelors who have had a difficult time finding domestic brides (because of the reluctance of Korean women to live in the countryside, far from urban modernity). There are active state and social programs to assist in assimilating foreign brides to "Korean cultures."[24] Yet Korean nationals abroad, including biracial Koreans, adoptees, Korean Chinese, North Korean refugees, Korean Americans, and Korean Japanese, have limited rights and privileges in South Korea.[25] This is despite a gradual warming to Koreans living abroad and foreigners living in Korea because of the need for global networks since the Asian financial crisis and the Kim Dae Jung era of economic liberalization.[26] These radical changes, such as the Korean state's multicultural policies and inclusive attitudes toward non-normative nationals, arose from the need to promote reproduction and population control in the context of the global capitalist competition for human resources. They have resulted in the sidelining and trivializing of populations that do not contribute—including women who are reluctant to participate as or be reduced to the reproductive machinery of the Korean capitalist nation-state.[27]

Contexts of Rental Housing, Financializations, and Affect of Enjoyment

With the new emphasis on reproduction, the locations and issues of unmarried women have been further trivialized. However, young unmarried women who want to live by themselves and enjoy their lives without rushing to marry or ever marrying at all are the embodiment of a liberal persona that eulogizes "enjoyment" as a life-governing principle. They enunciate and approximate the ideal of an unbridled life in the pursuit of individual realization and free from family and customary bonds. This is the kind of life that becomes more and more an asset and a commodity within the neoliberal economy in the rubric of flexibility that serves to navigate unstable, unpredictable, and competitive job markets. The ideal, one that cannot be fully achieved but is still pursued, is to be capable of maneuvering between a free lifestyle grounded in a private living place and the requirements of flexible labor, for which people must become equipped with self-management skills and financial techniques. Chapter 3 illustrates the way in which these unmarried women adopt and embody the affect of "enjoyment" as a life-governing principle. However, as Chapter 2 demonstrates, because of expensive rents, it is hard for them to afford a full-fledged liberal urban life. The majority of the unmarried women I interviewed in Seoul and Busan, the two largest cities in South Korea, cannot afford to own a house or condominium.[28] Only two of the thirty-five women I interviewed managed to own permanent housing: one because she inherited a public housing apartment from her late mother and the other because she lived alone in her parent's place, as their business had gone bankrupt and they were avoiding being traced by loan lenders.

As a result, I focus here on residential rental housing and some public housing but not on property ownership. In the South Korean context, owning a place is a cultural-historical custom for establishing a household—for the working class as much as for the middle class. Rental housing has been the primary form of residence for the working poor and only a temporary form of residence for the middle class—on their way to house ownership. Among the rental housing options, I concentrate on the predominant rental system of the yearly lease, the *chônse*, and its variations, including a significant variation involving both a lease and monthly payments (*chonwôlse* or *wôlse*). Chapter 2 elaborates on the connection between the lease system and the financial markets in that the rental system is a saving mechanism from the perspective of tenants and a credit-loan opportunity from the perspective of landlords.

If the rental system is an embellishment of the pre–Asian financial crisis era lump-sum cash transaction that took place in informal speculative financial sectors, financial know-how (*chaetekû*) is a marker of the new kinds of speculative financial life that began to flourish in formal sectors that have become dominant since the crisis. After the crisis, credit cards and the mortgage system were popularized, and all sorts of financial institutions (for instance, banks; stock-trading companies; and venture capital, bond, insurance, and credit card companies) competed with each other to attract individual clients. This is the time when, despite the generalization that "Asian prudence" was a problem for the global economy, The Economist (2009) noted that

> South Korea is an exception to the rule of Asian prudence. Its households' debt amounts to 150 per cent of disposable income, even higher than in America. The banking system, which borrowed heavily abroad to finance a surge in domestic lending, has also been badly hit by the global credit crunch, making it harder for firms to finance investment.[29]

While The Economist's evaluation of Korean exceptionalism indicates the extent to which South Korea magnified credit circulation, it is not yet clear how and why Korean households' loan and credit practices became so highly intensified historically. The concept of financialization is a useful tool to use in situating the Korean financial market's impact on households' management. At the same time, financialization is an essential concept in rethinking the significance of the informal financial economy and the history of money capital in the household economy. When financialization is used to refer to the invasion of formal financial commodities (banks, insurance, and credit card companies) into the household economy, the Korean case reveals that future investment (and speculation) was present in the informal sectors even before the launch of the formal sectors after the Asian financial crisis. Studies on financialization describe this aspect of global finance coming down to the household level as new, which is true in terms of the scope and speed of global financial exchange through advanced communication media. It is also new that household economy has been pulled into speculative profit making in the financial market, if we think in the context of advanced capitalist nations, where banks have been central financial institutions that households, as well as industry, have relied on for saving and borrowing since the beginning of industrial capitalism.

Thinking about the informal financial sector might appear to be useful only in the nonwestern context, but the majority of the world's households—both inside and outside advanced capitalist nations—have never had sufficient household income, especially when relying on a single breadwinner's wage from so-called secure employment. Furthermore, as Ananya Roy (2005) aptly notes, informality operates as a mode, or way of thinking, rather than a sector that implies a clear boundary. In particular, the informal economy has been crucial both for the subsistence of working poor and for the flexible accumulation of the capitalist system.[30] What might be a missing link, which I attempt to uncover, is the way in which the informal sector and markets (along with kin resources and social networks' in-kind capital) have contributed to financialization in their own way or in conjunction with formal sector-led financialization. The Korean case is an effective window because formal financial markets were never favorable to households until global finance's arrival through the Asian financial crisis.

In this context, I call the custom of credit and speculation in the informal mode (rotating credit associations, private loans, rental housing practices, and money gift exchanges in social networks) "sedimented financialization," and I call credit and speculation in the formal mode (banks, insurance, stock markets, and credit cards) "global financialization." The commonality between the two kinds of financialization is the explanatory power that money capital is central to the logic of asset accumulation, whether it is at the household level or the national/global level. This is the belief that money makes money, the assumption that money is the most rewarding means of asset management and growth in the capitalist market. This book considers that there is some truth to the belief that making interest through money capital is a crucial means of asset accumulation, because it has been established through street wisdom and the mundane practices of workers and subalterns.[31] This is in spite of my building on the criticism of money capital as "fictitious" capital by many critical political economists, including Marx and his followers. They argue that some money capital, called finance capital, especially interest-bearing capital (interest that is invested in further accumulation) and credit capital (money that is loaned by speculating on future worth, with the risk of failure), do not have real value because they do not contain the corresponding value of the materialized commodity. These thinkers deem wages from industrial production the only true source of capitalist accumulation.[32]

Chapter 2, delineating rental housing (chônse) and financial know-how (chaetekû) as windows of sedimented and global financialization, respectively, draws out the implications of them regulating single women's housing, economic independence, and life security. It is clearly a gendered and classed regulation of asset growth mechanisms that discriminates against single households. Further, these financial investment techniques (through rental housing and later through the development of speculation in formal financial markets) need critical attention in order to understand the South Korean capital accumulation process. Until now, Korean capitalism has predominantly been explained through the framework of the "developmental [capitalist] state," with the Korean state and big conglomerates (chaebôl) the two pillars leading the accretion of national profits through industrial production.[33] However, as noted above, it is important to consider the theoretical contribution of thinking about the informal mode for the history of financialization (grounding the survival strategies of subalterns), not just in Korea but on a global scale. This would involve a more nuanced understanding at the level of the household economy of irregular income earners' management of life security and asset growing (through mostly informal financial markets) and an analysis of their contribution to the macro level of national and global revenue generation and the reproduction of the capitalist system. The difficulty in quantifying the informal economy should not be a reason for dismissing its significance.

The financial practices that involve speculating about the most lucrative or economically wise actions do not take place apart from ethical practices. According to Michel Foucault (1988, 1998), people's ethical concerns for how to govern and care for themselves, what he terms "technologies of the self," are obscured by the morality of asceticism. He notes:

> We are more inclined to see taking care of ourselves as an immorality, as a means of escape from all possible rules. We inherit the tradition of Christian morality which makes self-renunciation the condition for salvation. To know oneself was, paradoxically, a means of self-renunciation. . . . Since the sixteenth century, criticism of established morality has been undertaken in the name of the importance of recognizing and knowing the self. Therefore, it is difficult to see the care of the self as compatible with morality. "Know thyself" has obscured "Take care of yourself" because our morality, a morality of asceticism, insists that the self is that which one can reject. (Foucault 1998, 228)

Further, both financial and ethical practices are not just reducible to individual matters; they are also circulated through popular sentiments and public discourses. As chapters 1 and 2 show through the single women's narratives, concerns about financial management skills are coupled with the women's understanding of how to care for themselves in the process of achieving residential autonomy and an antiestablishment lifestyle. At the same time, the women's desires and reflections are shaped by macro-historical changes.

The liberalization of finance and the economy followed the liberalization of the Korean polity, which got its start in the late 1980s and early 1990s with the historic end of the military dictatorship (Ogle 1990). That is the period when my research participants contributed to the democratic victory as rank-and-file student activists. The new liberal atmosphere was embodied in the political realm, which featured a strengthened women's movement, civil society movements (*simin sahoe undong*), and human rights movements that focused on such issues as the rights of political prisoners, adoptees, migrant workers, same-sex relationships, and people with disabilities. The liberal social ethos of seeking individual freedom and independence came to prevail in a wide spectrum of socioeconomic realms, including the push for democracy in existing institutions (government, the media, business, the military, education, health, religious organizations), pioneering new life and working styles (dot.com companies, self-employment, expanded leisure and travel, child-care co-ops), and the popular "quality of life" rhetoric and consumption of "well-being" products (Song 2009b) by stressing a "less stressful life" or the significance of psychological health (Song forthcoming, Song and Lee forthcoming), along with liberalized financial market services and products.

Whether the formal student activists' spirit of opposition disappeared in the surge of civil society movements is a central question for Korean intellectuals searching for alternatives to neoliberal political and economic regimes (Tangdaebipyông 2008, 2009; Kyunghyang Sinmun Special Report Team 2008). Sometimes it seems as if there has been a clear rupture from the previous regime, as exemplified in chapter 1 by the way in which the play A Room of One's Own has been produced and presented in different eras in South Korea. At other times, the legacy of oppositional politics is not apparent in the research participants' conflicts and dilemmas concerning their relationships with activism. This political aspect is at the heart of the last two chapters, which discuss the (neo)liberal technology of the self (chapter 3) and conflicting affective domains (chapter 4).

What penetrates the social ethos and the socioeconomic realm is not just ideological propaganda. The social ethos is, rather, circulated through affective channels through the dominant public feeling. The affect that became dominant after liberalization is the imperative of enjoyment: the need for people to feel joy in their activities and in their ways of living and working and to nurture and develop their capacity to enjoy life and themselves. This is a counter movement to the predominantly emitted affect of the military era (pre-1997), which promoted a solemn, dutiful persona to go along with the "labor of social mourning," or people's shared feelings of grief during the dictatorship in South Korea.[34] There was a historic transition from the affective domain of class-based oppositional politics to identity-based plural politics.

Although social grieving was the predominant affect circulated through poetry and songs preoccupied with "death" during the mass demonstrations against the dictatorship, enjoyment emerged as the theme of the collective following the crisis. My research participants, who experienced both eras, understandably vacillate between these two affective realms (solemn feeling and enjoyment) in coping with the postcrisis era. More important, they use those affects, especially enjoyment, as a means of self-suspension—a moratorium on their lives—as well as an instrument of self-affirmation and life

building. This seemingly polarized and confusing sentiment is necessary in
the process of developing a new social ethos for self and social governing.
Chapter 4 traces these competing affective domains in the single women's
narratives.

In the chapters that follow, chapter 1 introduces various single wom-
en's accounts of how they left their parents' homes to settle in their own
places, despite the discriminatory and discomfiting realities of marriage pressure and patriarchal sexual control of women in South Korea. Chapter 2
contextualizes the institutional and economic challenges to single women
attempting to live on their own and situates single women's financial insecurity in the historical context of sedimented and global financializations.
Chapter 3 addresses the affective realm that influences the generation of
former student activists, centering on the imperatives of enjoyment embodied in the lives and environments of single women. It features the ironic
convergence of enjoyment as an antiestablishment affect and enjoyment as
an attribute of neoliberal self-management. Chapter 4 wraps up the book
by focusing on how the affective influence from the preliberalization era is
maintained in single women's activities in political and social organizations.

CHAPTER I

Journey to a Room of One's Own

* ◆ •━━━━━• ◆ •

A woman must have money and a room of her own. . . . At the thought
of all those women working year after year and finding it hard to get
two thousand pounds together, and as much as they could do to get
thirty thousand pounds, we burst out in scorn at the reprehensible
poverty of our sex. What had our mothers been doing then that they
had no wealth to leave us? . . . thinking of the safety and prosperity
of the one sex and of the poverty and insecurity of the other and of
the effect of tradition and of the lack of tradition upon the mind of a
writer, I thought at last that it was time to roll up the crumpled skin
of the day, with its arguments and its impressions and its anger and its
laughter, and cast it into the hedge.

—Virginia Woolf, *A Room of One's Own,* 1929 (italics added)

A Room of One's Own, the well-known essay by Virginia Woolf, satirizes
male-dominated British intellectual society and asserts the need for women's
spatial and economic independence. A dramatization of *A Room of One's
Own* (*Chagi man ŭi pang*) has been a central text in the feminist the-
ater movement in South Korea since 1992. The play employs the satiric,
Enlightenment style of the original work but reconstructs the content for
the Korean context.

The changes in the play over the last two decades reflect transforma-
tions in the South Korean political ethos and in South Korean feminism.
In the early 1990s, the piece focused on a critique of South Korean male
intellectuals who were notorious for denigrating or patronizing women in

their writing and theory.[1] The narrator was an indignant woman whose antagonism to patriarchal power resonated with the oppositional political movement that sought to bring an end to the military dictatorship. The 2007 version of the production showed a dramatic shift in focus and narrative style. Instead of criticizing the views of male intellectuals, it focused on women's space and women's bodies, particularly the womb, which was used as a metaphor for the universe. Yi Yông-nan, the producer and actor, noted that the new version promoted inner harmony for individual women rather than a collective confrontational approach to the status quo.[2]

This transition from a socially antagonistic rhetoric to an individual-centered, harmonious discourse reflects the historic political change that took place in South Korea in 1987 when electoral democracy was established after three decades of Cold War military dictatorships. The political change was accompanied by a tremendous growth in civil society movements (Moon 2002; K. T. Park 2008), giving rise to a women's movement, environmental activism, consumer movements, and human rights movements for sexual minorities, adoptees, migrant workers, and people with disabilities. Before democratization, the predominant sociopolitical movements populated by university students, peasants, and workers organized potent collective demonstrations against state oppression (Koo 2001; N. Lee 2005; Nam 2009). Although the post-1987 civil society movements still highlighted solidarity among these different groups, individual interests and the spirit of independent entrepreneurism came to be seen as a prominent element of democracy throughout the 1990s (Abelmann 1996), especially during and after the Asian Financial Crisis from 1997 to 2003 (Seo 2009; Song 2007, 2009b). In chapters 3 and 4, I consider the way in which this political transition affected public feeling and people's attitudes about how life should be—in particular, that life should be enjoyable. In this chapter, I want to address the concrete consequences of the political transition in the lives of single women, especially the process by which they become single household dwellers.

Sexual Moral Regime

Korean women are expected to live with their parents before marriage because of customary traditions (as well as the high cost of urban housing, as I demonstrate in chapter 2). Single women living apart from their parents are considered unusual in South Korea, where women are seen as belonging to their fathers until they are married (Deuchler 1992; Haboush 1991; Janelli and Janelli 1982). The neo-Confucian convention was solidified in the last Korean dynasty (1392 to 1910). It dictates parents' responsibility to protect and supervise their unmarried daughters' sexualities.[3] Surprisingly, this continues in spite of the wide exposure to and popularity of cosmopolitan culture through travel and the mass media and the fact that more women consider marriage to be optional than in the past.[4] The convention continued even when neo-Confucianism, as well as other religions—such as Buddhism and aboriginal shamanism—began to lose their force as western religions, most significantly Protestantism and Catholicism, became more widespread in Korea.[5] Christianity itself is founded on a conservative gender norm that recognizes sex for procreation within a conjugal relationship as the only legitimate sexuality.[6] In addition, the predominant Christian denomination in South Korean development was led by fundamentalist Protestants, making any reversal of the age-old convention highly unlikely.[7] Sojông, a single woman in her early thirties, shared her experience:

> Among older generations, there is certainly a prejudicial perception of unmarried women not living with their parents—the sense that their life is undisciplined and that they are sexually promiscuous [grin]. So people are uneasy about single women not living with their parents in the marriage market or match-making context. I met an older auntie who used to quite adore me at my sister's wedding. She chastised me for telling people that I live alone and said that rather I should tell them that I'm living with a sibling or my parents [another grin].

Chunhee, a single woman in her early thirties, reveals her parents' continuing surveillance even when she lived in a college residence:

> If I wasn't there to get their phone calls in the evening, or there were signs of me sleeping over at someone else's, the whole family went crazy. So I ran away. They were so mad at me and I was angry with them.

Most of the women I interviewed do not submit to the conventional norms that regulate women's sexuality and residence; rather, they resist them. Their forms of resistance vary, depending on the extent of marriage pressure they receive and their own positions on marriage. Some forms of resistance are subtle, like Sojông's grin. In other cases, the resistance is more pronounced. For example, Chunhee ran away from her parents, so they negotiated to send her to study English in Canada. In short, South Korean single women who dream of the freedom of adulthood, including being able to live on their own, are active agents of liberal self-governing practices that compete with the conservative sexual moral regime. They are on the battleground of moral governance.

It is nothing new for Korean women to struggle and negotiate between a conservative moral regime and a more liberal one. Without those struggles since the early twentieth century, the legal achievement and slow social acceptance of gender equity in education, the vote, political leadership, art production, economic power, and cosmopolitan cultural exposure would not have occurred.[8] Of course, gender equity has by no means been achieved. But what is new since the late 1980s and the end of the dictatorship is the impact of popularized liberal ideas, desires, and practices on ordinary women's daily lives. Certainly, an attempt to have their own space was not a prevalent social phenomenon among unmarried women under the previous era's rigid political, moral, and cultural rubric.[9]

To be fair, some Korean women sought a life outside the institutions of marriage and family in the 1920s and 1930s. They were known as "new women" or "modern girls," like similar women in other Asian countries and on the global scene.[10] Images of well-educated women exercising their free will appeared again briefly in the short-lived liberal regime of the late 1950s while the country recuperated from the Korean War (1950–1953) and before the first military dictatorship was established in the early 1960s.[11] Yet these precursors were few and far between. Unmarried women trying to live a life of freedom only became widespread much later, when freedom of travel abroad became permitted in 1989. This enabled not only upper middle class people but many young working-class adults (including college students from working-class families) to travel. A number of my informants backpacked in Europe, Australia, and Mexico or studied English and/or visited relatives in North America. Young people without much economic power could seek new experiences and freedom by choosing the cheapest travel options in the growing competitive market of travel agencies.[12] My research participants proudly shared these experiences as evidence that their pursuit of individual development and cosmopolitan experience were similar to their young male peers.

Another example of the popularization of the liberal environment that affected young single women is their exposure to contemporary foreign films, especially Hollywood films and TV series,[13] through the mass media, which grew and was fully liberalized during the Asian financial crisis. (The market was deregularized as a condition of restructuring the economy.) Although Hollywood films were introduced into South Korea in the 1950s and some old U.S. TV series, such as MASH and Dynasty, were shown in Korea, American TV series were only introduced en masse after the crisis (McHugh and Abelmann 2005). My informants commonly mentioned Sex and the City, Will and Grace, Queer as Folk, Ally McBeal, Grey's Anatomy, and CSI. Even before the crisis, from the beginning of the liberal era in the early 1990s, there was an increasing opportunity to watch foreign films in new independent film festivals, including women's film festivals and queer film festivals.[14] These were initially begun in universities but came to be more widely held, with corporate and government sponsorship. During and after the crisis, it became common for municipal governments to host major film festivals, such as the Seoul Women's Film Festival, the Chônju Independent Film Festival, the Puchôn Fantastic Film Festival, and the Busan International Film Festival.[15] The single women I interviewed were almost all ardent fans of Hollywood TV dramas and a regular part of the audience at the film festivals. Many of them were volunteers or temporary employees at those festivals.

In addition to cultural liberalization, women's rights and conscious-raising movements reached their peak after democratization, in the early 1990s. During this period the first A Room of One's Own was performed, establishing the legend for the following decade. The local women's movement was reinforced by the global women's movement's promotion of the "mainstreaming of gender equality" (in politics and government leadership) and the Beijing conference in 1995.[16]

Although unmarried women played a central role in the leadership and staff of the women's movement throughout the gender mainstreaming era, ironically, single women's issues emerged very slowly (see chapter 4 for a more detailed discussion of these issues). Unmarried women attempted to address the marginalization by creating and circulating a new category of single women: pihon yôsông, meaning literally "unmarried," but with the added connotation of being "unassociated with marriage." Pihon yôsông includes women who are not legally married, regardless of whether they have a significant other, and divorced women. This new term is to be distinguished from the more conventional labels of "not-yet-married women" (mihon yôsông) and "never-married women" (toksin yôsông). These newly defined single women are the audience for and supporters of the feminist Pihon Yôsông Festival, founded in 2007, and other progressive women's media and labor organizations.[17]

Thus, my research participants, identifying as pihon yôsông, were armed with a new identity for the battle against social norms, spearheading women's residential liberation as an individual action but also as part of a collective consciousness and public feeling. Not only did they go through these particular social historical moments (cosmopolitan cultural influence through media and travel and mainstreaming of gender equality) with other South Koreans, my research participants had also been student activists throughout democratization and the liberalization of social movements, refocusing their political attention on women's issues and other social justice issues. Thus, their journey to live in their own dwellings as unmarried women and their efforts to be connected to social movements are signs of both liberal and leftist personae.

It is not much of an exaggeration to say that unmarried women without family support still had few options apart from being homeless, both
symbolically and literally. The courageous praxis of liberal and leftist ide-
ologies represented by many pihon yôsông such as my research participants
have had precedence from the early twentieth century in Korean history
(before the division of Korea into North and South), when the country
begun systemizing antifeudal polity and law. Na Hye-sôk, a liberal pioneer
"new woman" artist in the 1920s to 1930s, became homeless and socially
ostracized after divorcing and being vocal about the patriarchal subjection
of women in marriage.[18] She died of hunger and cold. Kang Kyông-ae, a
socialist woman writer in the 1920s and 1930s, wrote about proletarian
women's impoverished life outside of the institution of marriage. Even following liberalization in the late 1990s, when during the Asian financial
crisis many women became homeless, they were not considered such by
government workers. They were not imaginable as homeless, but if they had
to be categorized, they were seen either as immoral mothers who left home,
abandoning their children, or as sex workers, who were morally unacceptable
(Song 2009b). The single women who benefited from liberal policies and
discourses and became more bold and willing to try new paths in the new
millenium, such as my research participants, had to deal with their sense
of insecurity and fear of becoming "homeless" when they do not choose to
be or happen to be aligned with the institution of marriage.[19]

Despite the fear of being in poverty or homeless because of not getting
into marriage, it was, ironically, family pressure to marry more than anything
else that motivated my research participants. The constant matchmaking
discussions and the invasive comments about their appearance intended
to make them more suitable for the marriage market were part of most of
the women's experience. For example, Pohûi, an unmarried woman in her
mid-thirties, said:

> My mom said constantly, "Don't you have a boyfriend? Aren't you
> going to get married? Why do you live like that [without having
> a boyfriend], unlike a young woman? You must lose weight. If you
> are not going to marry, make enough money to live by yourself.
> What you make for working in the women's organization is like
> pocket money from a student's part-time job."

In the context of marriage being regarded as the guarantee of subsistence and economic safety for women (and also a morally legitimate destina-
tion), daughters who do not prioritize going into the marriage market—by
making efforts, for example, to have a feminine appearance and manner—
are objects of concern. Even more worrying is that some daughters do not

have the time or energy because they are "distracted" by working at low-income NGO jobs. In extreme cases, parents themselves have suggested that their "old maid" daughters move out in order not to lose face, because it is not just the women but their parents who risk becoming the object of pity from kin members and social networks (including church members, coworkers, neighbors, and friends). Although the individual women's economic and emotional relationships with their parents varied, their reliance on family for economic and moral support was fundamental, regardless of their resistance to family regulations. What follows are these women's stories of how they came to be living on their own.

Moving Out to Go to University in the City

One of the most common routes to single households for these young women is leaving home to attend university in big cities far from where their parents reside. More than half of my informants started living apart from parents as "students from the countryside" (chibang haksaeng), staying in boarding houses or places their parents arranged for them (sometimes with siblings). Eventually all of them ended up living by themselves when they graduated from university or when their siblings left to marry or to take a job in another location. According to Wony, a single woman in her late thirties who went to Seoul from a southern city and lived by herself for ten years:

> Marriage has been the issue that my parents nagged me about most. The first four to five years were really tough. But living apart from them really helped me. If I see them, it's hard to bear. My mom's personality is quite strong. She always makes comments on the way I talk and behave, or my clothing style. So, I had a really hard time to find out what I like or want to do because I spent more time on how to make my mom understand and fighting with her all the time. It is painful even visiting home occasionally for holidays.
>
> I think marriage pressure is the biggest reason why single women in their late twenties or early thirties want to get out of their parents' place. But my parents would not allow me to move out unless I got married. That's why I chose to do my master's degree in Seoul. I think very highly of unmarried [women] friends whose parents live in Seoul, but they still managed to leave home and live by themselves. Can you imagine how difficult the process would have been for them? It probably matters less if they can afford to live on their own. But if not, if they need their parents' support to pay for rent, then it would be enormously hard.

Wony lived with a friend for a while in order to rely less on her parents for her rent deposit (*pojŭng'gŭm*), but she eventually moved out on her
own. Although she weighed her economic reliance on her parents as almost
as difficult an issue as emotional attachment in terms of her autonomy, she
found the emotional distance more challenging:

> While I was living apart from my parents, there was a brief period
> of getting their support for living expenses. They constantly scru-
> tinized my life through phone calls. They seemed to think they
> were entitled to know everything because they were paying for
> my living expenses. Then, over time, I began tutoring and took
> over my own living expenses. Of course, even so, I still needed
> my parents' support for situations that require a large lump sum
> (*moktton*), such as tuition and, more important, the rent deposit.
> I've paid back more than half of the rent deposit by now. After I
> started paying them off and taking care of my living expenses, I
> was able to distance myself somewhat from my parents and they
> had less control. However, I feel I'm only 80 percent self-reliant
> because I'm not emotionally independent from my parents. . . .
> The toughest part of living alone is to make significant decisions,
> such as repairing the apartment or negotiating the rent deposit.
> My parents used to make those decisions when I lived with them.
> I know I have to do it but I still have an expectation that some-
> one else should do those decision-making things for me. I ended
> up leaving things unrepaired. Also, my parents are still relying on
> me. If my parents get ill, I have to support them. If that happens,
> I cannot keep my current lifestyle.

Wony left home with the excuse of going away to school, but Sojŏng,
the single woman whose grin signaled her less pronounced resistance, did
not plan to live alone at first. She is also from the countryside. She left her
parents' hometown as a successful student entering a prestigious university in
Seoul. Initially, her departure was not associated with marriage pressure. She
began living in a place her parents had arranged for herself and her siblings.
She was left alone after her siblings were married. She lived alone for five
years, during which time she started getting heavy pressure to marry. She
said, "my parents would not have allowed me to move out if they had lived
in Seoul [grin]. I would have tried leaving anyway around the age I am now.
But I would have had to give up living alone within a few months without
their economic support." She is a rare case among my research participants of
a single woman who graduated from a first-tier university. A freelancer who

translates films, her income is irregular and her housing is fully financed by her parents. She wants to be a cosmopolitan, stylish single woman and to make more money, but she is not confident that she can achieve economic autonomy. More important, she dreads angering her parents:

> I'm anxious because I am economically unstable [grin]. When I quit my first job at a press after a year-long employment, I spent the money I had saved to prepare to be a freelance translator. But the payments for translations were paid awfully late and unpredictably—between a few months and a year after the job was done.[20] I can survive for a few months on the savings, but I wonder if I can do this freelancing over the long term for the next few decades. I'm not confident of getting a regular office job. Compared with my sister, who entered university a few years earlier than I did, my job situation is much worse.[21] She quit her job and went backpacking in Europe because she expected to get a job without much hassle when she returned from her trip. *But I never had such luxury or optimism* [grin]. People like me who graduated in the middle of the crisis don't have any prospects of getting a stable job. But still, there is peer pressure to be successful, cool women in terms of not only having good jobs but of being stylish. I think this emphasis on style and appearance is influenced by *Sex and the City*. It is a matter of whether you are good at self-management. If you are not pretty, it is not just a dis-advantage but a sign of being a loser and unable to manage yourself. It is hard to live up to both expectations of getting a stable job and being a stylish single woman. . . . I do not think I am emotionally independent from my parents. *It is not that I am depending on them but that I cannot object to what they expect.* More than anything, the marriage pressure opened up a big chasm between my parents and me. I have to laugh about my situation because I'm not saying I'd never marry but just that I want to marry when I feel like it—and it's not like I'm going to wait until I'm fifty. But it doesn't make sense to them at all. I get devastated when my parents get upset with me. Actually I feel worse when I find them being hurt than when I see them angry at me. For example, we never fight, but since my mom began pressuring me to marry, we had the first awkward moment of phone conversation. After the uneasy phone call, my mom did not pick up my calls for two days. I couldn't handle the psychological rejection from my mom. I'm not confident that I'll change my parents' minds, but I wonder whether they would be more understanding if I made more money [grin]. (italics added)

Moving out When Parents Live in the Same Area

Wony and Sojông do not think living alone would have been possible if their parents had lived in the same city. However, a few of my research participants managed to do it. Chisu is a self-identified lesbian in her mid-thirties who has lived by herself more than ten years.[22] Although marriage pressure was the tacit reason that she moved out, she justified leaving with the excuse of her intense workload at her job. She did not mention her lesbian identity during my interview as a reason for resistance to marriage or as a reason for moving out, although she made a connection between her identity and her job security as a primary concern of a single woman dwelling alone.

Chisu is a contract lecturer in a private after-school. Since the liberalization of the education system in South Korea in the late 1990s, many tutors and teachers work as temporary contract and part-time workers (S. J. Park and Abelmann 2004). In the context of the neoliberal job market—with a reduction in stable jobs and an expansion of unstable or precarious jobs—after-school private education is one of the major job markets that was expanded and primarily taken up by part-time or irregular women workers. Chisu's job is irregular in that there are no benefits, pension, or insurance, but the pay is relatively high. Regardless, her experience of living with her parents until she moved out is not much different from the experience of Wony, the single woman who moved away from her parents in the countryside with the excuse that she was going to university in a different city:

> My parents initially objected to me living alone. They think unmarried women's living away from their parents is deviant (chôngsang chôk iji anta) and dangerous (tongnip haesô sal myôn wûihôm hada) because they don't get their parents' protection. However, it wasn't like I felt protected by them when I was living in their place. It's rather an economic reason. However, marriage pressure got more intense after the Asian financial crisis. . . . After I turned twenty-eight—you know, after the so-called marriage age (kyôlhon chôngnyông'gi)—my parents felt very uncomfortable. Sometimes my parents got upset with me after relatives visited or after returning from extended family gatherings. They yelled at me, "Why do we have to hear such condescending comments from them [relatives]? They wonder what's wrong with you that you're not married and whether you have a deficiency." I, too, was stressed out by seeing my parents being hassled. Then they gave me two options: either get married or go abroad so that I am out of their and the relatives' sight. So I went abroad to learn English. Moving out felt so good because I didn't get pressure to marry. Especially after my parents

found that this job I'm in pays well, they seem to think that I'm economically stable and do not mention marriage that much. I feel fantastic about not being pushed to go on dates with guys arranged through matchmakers. Also, I don't have to avoid running into my relatives when they visit. My mom used to ask me if I had anywhere to go because my aunties were coming by.

When I asked Chisu if she felt the situations to be intrusive or violent, she answered:

> I took it as my mom being considerate. She basically says, "Aren't you going to be uncomfortable if the aunties visit today? Why don't you go to somewhere like the library and come back after they leave? They'll leave around such and such a time." Anyway, I myself didn't want to be home when the aunties dropped by.

After she moved out, her parents visited her place once a month and she visited them for holidays. She was very busy at work and barely had a day to rest on the weekend. She was sympathetic to her parents' situation but considers herself independent from her family, both emotionally and economically. She thinks that economic independence from her parents saved her from marriage pressure.

Chisu's excuse to move out from her parents' home was her work, but Hosôn, another single woman in her late thirties who had lived alone for two decades while her parents lived in the same precinct, made no excuses, neither work nor education. She simply moved out because she wanted to. Hosôn is the woman whose narrative (on the difficulty of society taking single women's issues seriously in the context of social anxiety about low fertility) I quote in the introduction. After being a music tutor for young children for a decade or so, Hosôn began marketing through the Internet. Neither job gave her economic stability. She openly revealed her vacillation between confidence and insecurity about living alone. She left her parents' home in her mid-twenties, abruptly announcing that she was moving out when the family was planning to move to a commutable suburb. When I asked her why, she said,

> I didn't want to live with my parents. I hated so much seeing my parents' disputes. I had put up with enough by then. My mom was the breadwinner, but living with my father has been very hard for her. My father is very temperamental and drinking all the time. So there was no peace at home. What made it unbearable was to witness my mom deteriorating because of this environment over the years. I loathed the situation. I wanted to be free of the environment.

Because I am the oldest child, I felt I was neglecting my obligation [to take care of parents and family].[23] However, when I let it go, I felt so liberated. I think I was really right to move out then. I enjoy my life so much; it's full of things I like to do. My friends and I, we say that around our age, we must move out. People who haven't moved out say they are frustrated with themselves and brood about how to make a move-out happen. I feel truly liberated. Although my parents weren't intervening much in my life when I lived with them, *I noticed a big difference between liberty under watching eyes and liberty without them.* (italics added)

Hosôn was not as pressured to marry as others I interviewed, and her motivation for moving out was not directly related to her parents' attempts to control her morally and sexually. However, her connection to her mother and her interactions with the family and relatives made her very self-conscious about not being married:

I felt shocked by some changes in my family dynamics after my younger siblings got married. I used to be very self-confident, at least in front of my family and relatives, because my mom trusted me and said I needed to live my life as I wanted. Then, within a year or so after my two siblings got married, my mom felt sorry for me and treated me as an object of pity in the eyes of relatives. It made me so discouraged and withdrawn. So even though I am a cheerful and respectful person whom all my relatives like, I stopped going to relatives' gatherings and even my mom's birthday dinner. That [not going to my mother's birthday dinner] upset my brother and sister quite a bit. I just said that I was busy. I surprised myself. I guess it was a very insecure and timid act, which is not really who I am or at least who I used to be. But I just did not want to join the parties. There are only married couples at the family gatherings. And my mom would feel pity for me. So I didn't want to see them [trembling voice] because I didn't want to be shaken by it. Seriously, if I see my mom or family, I can't control my emotion. The more I hear what my mom thinks of me, the harder I become on myself. So I avoid seeing and listening to her in order to live in peace.

When I asked Hosôn what she thought of marriage, she said:

I used to ignore the very thought of marriage. But recently I am becoming less adamant about it. I want someone to be in love with me. You know, people keep asking whether I'm not lonely, especially after I reached thirty years old. I've said no to that confidently so far. Even now, if people ask me, I can say "not lonely" more easily than "lonely." However, I ask myself again and again whether it's true, whether I'm really not lonely. Then, I answer myself, it's true that I'm a bit lonely. So, I have noticed a change inside me. I just want to have a person I can talk to about what I'm struggling with or to whom I can express my emotion.

Hosôn's trajectory challenges Wony's assumption that it is almost impossible for a single woman not to live with parents if they are in the same area unless she is earning a high salary. Hosôn's economic stability is no greater than that of Wony (or of Sojông, who also doubted the feasibility of moving out into the same city). But Hosôn left without hesitation when she knew what she needed and wanted (living in peace). Maybe Hosôn is "unusual" in that she was able to put her thought into action without feeling obliged to follow convention. However, her emotional vulnerability to her family and her efforts to distance herself from them is not unusual at all. What pressured Hosôn to change her feelings about marriage was her mother's pity and concern. Her soul searching about whether or not she was lonely shows how other people's preconceptions motivated her to identify her desires for a romantic relationship and to conflate the desire with a reconsideration of marriage. Thus, although the physical distance afforded by moving away from home helps unmarried women keep an emotional distance from family, their emotional susceptibility to the family remains challenging.

Moving out at Odds

Some women seek an alternative network or community to compete with the force of the family.[24] Minsô is unique in terms of her trajectory and her way of dealing with marriage and ties to family. Minsô came to live alone accidentally. While she was in college, her father decided to retire from his life-long employment. He was in his fifties. According to Minsô, he finally decided to live life for himself, which shocked and inspired her at the same time. Her parents announced that they were leaving Seoul in order to relocate to a country farmhouse. She and her brother lived together for three years until he was married, and then she lived on her own. Although she considers it very fortunate, in her mind she thinks she would have moved out anyway.

Minsô was plotting to move out because she felt suppressed by her parents, like a subordinate who must follow orders and is punished for any violation. She described the context as "coercive familialism" (*kangje chôk kajokchuŭi*). Her litany of grievances included the presumption that she was expected to sacrifice everything for the family; the pressure to marry but at the same time the prohibition against dating; her parents' dependence on her academic performance for their own satisfaction (common among the post–Korean War generation); severe punishment for drinking, smoking, and violation of her curfew; prohibition of or inability to understand extensive time spent with non-family members, including student activists; and disapproval of her work in an NGO because of the low income. However, after she lived apart from them, her parents gradually changed. She said:

> In the past, they hated the idea of me staying over at someone else's house. Then, after I'd been living on my own, although they spotted me coming home drunk, they just said, "Don't go around too late!" It astounded me, because it's a sea change. I'm still nervous about being spotted by them, but they seem to think it's unavoidable. I even used to be beaten if I came home late and drunk. But now, they just say, "Please come home early," and "Please quit smoking." I mean, it's not an order any longer but just putting their opinion out there. It took at least three years for them to adjust to this change. When they first moved to the countryside, Mom used to visit my place once a month. But she's hardly doing that now. Although my parents have errands and come to Seoul a couple of times a month, they don't visit me. They used to stay over at my place, saying it's what families do (*kajok tôen tori*). But nowadays, they say it's uncomfortable for them to stay with me, because I sleep late and have an irregular lifestyle. So they just go back home on the train without stopping by my place.

Although she is very critical about familialism because of her own family experience, she clarified that she does not hate her family:

> When I used to work in a women's organization on the outskirts of Seoul, my coworkers thought I was a bit strange. I don't date, I'm not interested in marriage, and I am a workaholic with very low wages. They encouraged me to get married. When I told them I was not going to marry, they asked me what was wrong in my family. They thought the reason why I wasn't interested in marriage was because of a big problem in my family and that I hate my family members. It's not like that at all. I'm just trying to be true to my ideas. I have never thought of office work, marriage, family, or socially accepted norms seriously. I just don't feel I belong in that kind of life. It's not because I dislike my family. My relatives also

think of me as quite odd. A close relative cornered me, asking, "So, is it true you haven't been on a single date to find a marriage partner arranged by a matchmaker (matsôn)?" When I answered "That's right, I haven't," the relative was shocked and said, "How is it possible? Are you lying to me?" In the past, if I was chastised by those people because I wasn't meeting their expectations, well, it upset me. But now, it amuses me. So I'm throwing back jokes to them. . . . I heard a comic story that cracked me up. A comedian was asked, "What is the family to you?" He answered, "I would throw it out if no one was watching me" [smile].[25]

When I asked whether she feels that way about her family, she answered indirectly, sharing a reflection about the natal family versus the "chosen family":

I realized that even the most beautiful memory about the family is like a mortgage of guilt or someone's sacrifice, something like, my mom went through so much trouble for me; my father sacrificed his life for me. Touching memories about the family are mostly based on the recognition of family members' sacrifice. . . . I don't think living together in the same space necessarily makes a primary social network. To me, sharing a lifestyle and perspectives makes the network. But there tends to be a coercive expectation within the family just because of blood and regional connection. The birth family seems to follow the "principle of proper." In order to get out of the family boundary, my friends (chubyônin, literally meaning people existing in one's surroundings, but referring to close neighbors in this narrator's linguistic usage) and I made huge efforts to build a community. We are six people who used to live around the same neighborhood. Some are married to each other now. It took more than five years of living like a flock. We found each other to be communicative and on the same page by doing things together like travel, meals, and collective purchases. Although I do not want to bind us as a family, they are more like a chosen family. Even now that we live in different neighborhoods, we meet quite often, at least twice a week. We agreed on the creation of this kind of a community based on our similar observations about our poor fit in the natal family. Most important, we allow ourselves to be individuals. When someone heard that I was living communally, she asked me jokingly how I could live with other people when I'm such an eccentric person. I told her that I don't live with other members in the same unit. I can't even sleep with another person in the same bed. Making a community doesn't mean sharing everything, eating the same thing, doing the same thing, keeping the same sleeping schedule. It'd repeat the framework of natal family norms. If we follow the frame, we'll again generate an unhappy family [smile] that becomes a burden and generates guilt. I want to live alone and live in a community that respects my lifestyle.

After Moving Out

After moving out, young single women continue to be harassed by neighbors and coworkers because of their single lifestyle and sexuality. For instance, Nani, an after-school tutor (a temporary contract job) in her late thirties, did not want to be in the office at lunch hour, the daily gathering time for tutors, because her coworkers repeatedly tried to persuade her to get married. Her coworkers—mostly women in their late twenties who considered working to be a transitional activity on the way to getting married—told her that living alone was abnormal and commented loudly enough for her to hear that she must be "lesbian." Nani is, in fact, a self-identified lesbian woman, active in the underground queer movement, but she did not come out to her coworkers because of fear of social and job discrimination. Nani eventually quit the job for other temporary work as a coordinator of a local film festival, where people were less inquisitive about her personal life, although her salary and benefits were no more secure.

Chisu, the woman with the relatively high income in a competitive private after-school, is also a self-identified lesbian. As noted, she did not present her identity as a ground for moving out. However, she told me she would have risked losing her job if her identity was exposed:

> Although I'm economically stable now, if I am outed [as a lesbian], I risk being laid off immediately. I had a male colleague who is gay. There must be a noticeable incident. The rumor is that he harassed students at work. I can hardly believe the accusation of sexual harassment, though. Why would he do such a stupid thing? He was fired because of the rumor and he did not get any support from colleagues at all. That kind of exposure ruins your career and isolates you from your workplace.

South Korea does not have legal protection for sexual minorities such as gay, lesbian, bisexual, and transgendered people. A human rights commission established in 2001 included discrimination against "sexual orientation" in its mandate. However, that particular item was excluded in the 2007 revision of the commission's protections (along with family composition

and national origin), despite years of human rights activists' efforts (Kim
Y-S. 2007).[26] Thus, the authority of the commission is limited to advice.
Even when it included the clause protecting sexual minorities, it had no
legal authority. Although employers followed the commission's advice to re-
employ affected sexual minorities, it was difficult for the employees because
of the prejudice against them, and there was no way to take back the
exposure of their identities. Activists for same-sex–loving women noted in
my interviews that in general, working-poor lesbian women and "feminine-
looking" lesbians were most pressured to marry. During the crisis, however,
when the economic situation was dire, pressure was also put on many "mas-
culine-looking" lesbians. Some agonizingly debated getting married in order
to survive.[27] Chisu, who has a somewhat masculine appearance, confessed
that during the crisis

> I was paranoid that I would die of hunger when I was outed at
> work and to my parents. I was contemplating marriage, seriously.
> If I suppress my bodily suffering, choosing to marry and live with a
> guy (*kûnyang nun ttak kam ko salmyô nûn*), at least my body won't
> starve to death.

As lesbians, Chisu and Nani face particular difficulties in complying
with conventional sexual norms and marriage practices. But all unmarried
women living alone face challenges, regardless of their sexual orientation:
they are treated as children or disabled people and their sexual security is
threatened.

Chagyông is another private after-school teacher in her late thirties.
Chagyông encountered invasive questions and harassment not only from her
coworkers but from her students as well. Her students often offered to be
matchmakers and teased her for being unmarried and living alone. She tried
to rise above these moments by presenting herself as "hip single," a highly
capable and self-sufficient single woman (*hwaryô han sing'gu'l ira pul'lô tao*),
a discourse indebted to the mass media's heralding of professional women
who live alone as a new cultural breed.

Chagyông also encountered discrimination in her social network of
former student activists, many of whom were now married to each other.
Some of them, the men especially, addressed her as an immature person,
comparing her to a child, and condescendingly referred to her as a defective
(*haja ka in nûn*) adult. Married men in the circle would demonstrate their
authority by saying to her at gatherings that "children should go home" or
"children shouldn't interfere with our adult business." She confronted them,
saying, "Are you kidding me? Who is more capable here? You or me?" Over
the last few years, she had stopped receiving invitations from her social

network of former student activists and was only notified formally about
annual year-end parties.

The other single women I have already introduced relayed similar
experiences of being treated as less than adults by their families. Chisu is a
middle child, with an older sister and a younger brother, both married. Her
parents and siblings consider her to be less mature than they are, to the
point that she is left out of big family decisions and is merely informed after
the fact. Wony's mother described her as "more pitiful" (*ni ka tô pulssang
hada*) than the married women working at the bottom of the labor market
that Wony was interviewing for her research. Her mother clearly considers
her single household to be an unstable life. There was a similar context of
pity in Hosôn's narratives.

These women are also heavily scrutinized during the process of looking
for a place to live. Miyông, a graduate student in her mid-thirties, is a private
tutor and freelance writer trying to eke out enough money for her tuition,
housing, and living expenses. When she entered a real estate agency office
(*pudongsan chung'gaeso* or *pokttôkppang*) to look for a rental apartment, she
noticed a pink highlight in a map of the district where she was looking for
a place. When she showed interest in the highlighted area because it was
close to where she worked, the real estate agent discouraged her. When she
asked why, he explained that the area was *nagayo ch'on* (a residential village
of bar hostesses), an area inhabited by women who worked in the red-light
district or entertainment industry.[28] In describing the conversation, Miyông
chuckled and stated that the agent was a middle-aged man who genuinely
seemed to want to protect her because, he said, her appearance (modest
clothing and no makeup) did not look like a bar worker's. But both the
agent's marking of the district as a ghetto and being judged by her appearance made her uncomfortable.

Miyông also runs into her neighbors' judgments about her sexual morals. For instance, in monthly neighborhood meetings (*pansanghoe*),[29] neighbors always try to get her to talk about her job and her age. The housewife
next door never fails to peek into Miyông's unit when she is leaving her
place and the door is ajar. Miyông does not feel comfortable bringing in a
lone guest, especially a male, because of the neighbors' constant surveillance.

Miyông and others further spoke of "sexual safety" (*sông chôk anjôn
sông*) as a primary concern and challenge of living by themselves. Although
Miyông was irritated by her lack of privacy around her neighbors, their surveillance was one of the only things protecting her from exposure to sexual
intimidation. She cited, for example, her experience with male construction workers who were building a multiple-residence house just next to her
apartment and who continually glanced over at her place, especially when
male guests came over.

Miyông's concern for sexual safety was echoed by other research participants. Kyuri noted that the recent controversy about a serial killer (at the time I was doing the interviews) made her afraid to be out late.[30] Further, she felt uneasy about the way the media fuelled panic among women living alone. Although the serial killer was not necessarily attacking women living alone, Kyuri's opinion was that the media focused on this, criticizing the "careless" lifestyle of single women. Togyông, another interviewee, said her fear of theft and robbery was a side effect of the media emphasis on single women living alone as the most vulnerable targets of the serial killer.

Yoon is an interviewee who had lost her job and was living on her savings, along with wages from some occasional freelance work and from tutoring her sister's children. She told me about an experience of sexual harassment by a male neighbor who, whenever he was drunk, tried to open her apartment door. When she reported the incident to her landlord, he chastised her for not confronting the neighbor or reporting him to the police. She explained that she did not want to contact the police because it might have provoked the neighbor to harm her. She wanted to move but was unable to because of the difficulty of getting out of her lease, especially during the winter. Yoon noted that South Korea is not yet socially prepared to support sexual safety. She gave examples of obsolete suggestions for "how to prevent sexual violence" in a typical secondary school textbook: avoid unknown people at night, do not wear sexually stimulating clothes, and leave the door open when dating. These perceptions of sexual safety being focused on potential women victim's responsibility rather than the education of potential aggressors or the support of victims led her to feel that she could not rely on any social consciousness regarding sexual safety. She did small things to protect herself, such as leaving a pair of men's shoes or many pairs of shoes in her entrance so that strangers would not notice she was living by herself.

My research participants recognized the very different situation of men who move away from home before they marry. Chunhee noted:

> If an unmarried man leaves his parents' place to live alone, he is respected as an independent adult. Whereas if an unmarried woman leaves her parents' place, she is suspected of giving up marriage or having some reason for not being able to enter the marriage market.

Moving out into one's own place is actually encouraged for men, with no concern for sexual modesty or safety; it is a sign of men's readiness to enter the marriage market. Both Hosôn and Minsô said that their parents endorsed their brothers living by themselves as preparation for them to get married. This is because of a conventional wedding condition: the bridegroom provides the residence for the newlyweds; the underlying meaning is that women enter patrilineal households, not vice versa (Janelli and Janelli 1982; Kendall 1996).

This gendered perception and practice regarding dwellings for single people means that unmarried women are treated differently within their nuclear families. For example, Minsô said:

> My parents were trying to separate my living place from my brother's. They said the son should have his own place. Otherwise, no woman would be interested in marrying him. Although I told them it was not because of him not having his own residence [but because he wasn't very romantic], they were persistent. They suggested I move out, with a proposal to give me far less cash than I needed for deposit money to get my own place. It flipped me out because of their obvious son preference and discrimination against me, their daughter.

Kyuri, whose family is poverty stricken (her father had died from Agent Orange, to which he had been exposed as a soldier in the Vietnam War), summed up the options available to unmarried women in comparison to unmarried men:

> If unmarried women want to move out, their options are either poverty or marriage. For single men, though [chuckle], moving out is a less crucial choice. It means either the inconvenience of taking care of domestic chores on their own or marriage to resolve the inconvenience by letting their brides take care of domestic matters.

As the earlier part of this chapter notes, the fear of becoming homeless (with the historic precedence of Na Hyesôk and Kang Kyông-ae) has a practical basis, and marriage is the primary viable option if women do not want to be left in poverty.

The sexual regulation of single women in the family and in marriage is not just a matter of emotional support. The economic instability of unmarried women results in a heavy reliance on the family's financial support in order to acquire a place of their own.

Recurring statements in this chapter assert the power of money capital as the only option to replace social capital, which operates through the logic of reciprocity in the familial and kinship world and tends to be the primary source of receiving or borrowing lump-sum cash (see details in chapter 2). Pohûi, one of the single women who was pressured by her mom to date and get married, with nagging comments on her bodily shape and unjustified focus on her low-paying job, relays her mother's view: "If you are not going to marry, make enough money to live by yourself." Sojŏng, who also moved out and away from her family, said, "I wonder whether they would be more understanding if I made more money" [grin]. Chisu, one of the few single women who moved out from her parents' place when they lived in the same area, echoes the power of money to pacify family pressure: "Especially after my parents found that this job I'm in pays well, they seem to think that I'm economically stable and do not mention marriage that much."

Can individual unmarried women without sufficient money capital who do not want to rely on the familial network use bank loans? The next chapter answers this question by showing the way in which the heteronormative sexual and moral control of unmarried women is systematically embedded in housing, finance, and employment institutions.

Chapter 2

Unmarried Women's Housing and Financial Insecurities

* ❖ ⊢━━━━━━━⊣ ❖ *

I needed lump-sum cash (moktton) for moving out from my parents' house. My parents provided it to me. When I lived with a roommate, I used to pay half of the rent deposit for the apartment (chônse). Then she moved out, so I needed more lump-sum cash. I had to ask my parents, again very nervously, but fortunately they gave it to me. Over the last ten years, I have paid them back just over half. My rent deposit is about 40 million Korean won [US$40,000].[1] It is impossible to save that much money when I can barely pay my living expenses with the income of an unstable part-time job. I don't have financial know-how (chaetekû) or a good enough understanding of the economy (kyôngje kwan'nyôm). I don't know how to accumulate big money. Even though I happen to have some money saved, I don't know how to make it grow.

—Wony

South Korean urban housing is notoriously high-priced and difficult to obtain, partially because the economic development period (1960–1987) resulted in a high influx of the rural population into cities, where there were more job opportunities and better education than in rural areas. Seoul's metropolitan area is now the third most populous in the world after Tokyo and Jakarta (according to the World Atlas) and comprises almost half of South Korea's total population (48 million).[2] Seoul is approximately half the size of New York City, but it is about one-fifth more populous. In a situation of tight housing conditions, it is challenging for anyone without a good job, savings, or an affluent family to think of living on his or her own.

This aspect, in combination with the social norms that pressure unmarried women to live with their parents, might explain why it is so difficult for single women to move out. Yet there are more constraints and challenges beyond the basic fact of overpopulation in Seoul and other big cities in South Korea.

When Wony talks about how she had to borrow money from her parents, readers might wonder why a rent deposit is so expensive. Wony's narrative reveals at least three key words that significantly concern unmarried women in regard to housing and financial security in the context of the post–Asian financial crisis economy. Lump-sum cash (moktton) and the rental apartment system (chônse) were already in place before the crisis broke. However, with the crisis and the emerging discourses of financial know-how (chaetekû), unmarried women seeking a single household and, in fact, any South Koreans were affected with increasing anxiety and self-blame by this new and quickly changing financial environment.

When scholars see financialization as a key feature of neoliberalism or late global capitalism, they are usually referring to the use of financial tools, such as bonds, equity, stocks, and residential mortgages, as a way to mitigate the risk of economic loss undertaken by speculating on the future value of assets.[3] However, this device of mitigating the risk ends up creating more risks when the interest on credit increases far beyond the original amount and the resulting total debt cannot be paid with real value (whether wages or money). The recent U.S. subprime mortgage housing financial crisis is a good example.[4] Some see this financialization as similar to the rise of finance capital, which both Marx and Hilferding observed in the mergers conducted between industrial capitalists and financial capitalists to maximize profits in the late nineteenth century (Marx 1990, 1991; Lenin 1939; Hilferding 1981; Harvey 2005; Sunder Rajan 2006). Others see financialization differently—as more than just similar to early finance capital, in that it is not only corporate capital but also includes the money of individuals who are invested in the financial capitalist mechanism through pensions, mortgages, credit cards, and meticulously increasing service fees (Lapavitsas 2009, Martin 2002, Langley 2008, LiPuma and Lee 2004).

Lapavitsas (2009) defines the "financialization of everyday life" as the last-three-decades-old layer of financial capitalism in neoliberalism, built upon individual households' daily usage and need of credit and financial services. He notes that recent financialized capitalism is different from the early capitalism with finance capital to which Marx and others paid attention. However, in South Korea, the picture of financialization is more complicated, not only because of Korea's more recent development and late joining in the global free market but because of the heavy influence of informal financial markets since the end of the Korean War, long before the advent of neoliberalism. Some would argue that these informal scales and modes cannot be compared to formal scales and modes of financial speculation. But there is little difference in the logic and desire for speculation that will procure assets by privileging the circulation of money capital—especially seeking profits from interest making—rather than by the production of labor capital. The process of exploitation can be even more complex if one takes into account the fact that the informal market relies heavily on a primary social network, such as kin members and neighbors, as Elyachar (2010) succinctly points out. In this context, by distinguishing Lapavitsas's definition of financialization as "global financialization," I label the informal financial markets that are a profound infrastructure for household economy as "sedimented financialization."[5]

This chapter aims to outline these conceptual and historical distinctions—sedimented and global financializations—in terms of the magnifying effects of the combined systems on single women's lives as a window on a gendered group of the working-poor class. It provides a picture of how sedimented financialization has played a significant role in the prevailing literacy of speculating money capital even during the era known as the "Fordist mode of production" or "pre-neoliberal capitalism," with the effect of excluding the working poor, those without money capital. We can see that a kind of finance capital existed all along. And sedimented financialization does not just coexist with global financialization shaped through the formal financial market. Rather, sedimented financialization propels the new financialization with accelerated speed (of circulation), intensity (of anxiety), and effect (of polarization of financial classes) in the current moment of capitalism, as we see in South Korean quotidian practices.

These financial investment techniques (through rental housing and informal loans and, later, through exposure to global markets) need critical attention if we are to understand the South Korean asset accumulation process. Until now, Korean capitalism has predominantly been explained through the framework of the "developmental (capitalist) state," with the Korean state and big conglomerates (chaebôl) the two pillars leading the accretion of national profits through industrial production.[6] However, at the level of the household economy, a more nuanced understanding of irregular income earners' management of life security and asset growing through mostly informal financial markets is necessary.

Residential Options for Unmarried Women

Housing options for young single women are mostly limited to yearly leases and some monthly rentals. The majority of my research participants lived in small studio or one-bedroom rental apartments in Seoul or Busan. Exceptions include a woman who inherited public rental housing from her mother upon her mother's death; another who lives in a small apartment on the outskirts of Seoul that is owned by her parents, who are living separately to avoid being traced by creditors; a third who lives in a unit in a combined build-ing of office/residences called *opisûtel* (or office-tel, a mixture of offices and hotel rooms)[7]; and a fourth who lives in a commercialized boarding house for people who are preparing national exams, called *kosibang*. Their rented apartments ranged in size from 50 square feet to 300 square feet. The aver-age price my informants paid for a yearly lease was between $10,000 and $50,000. Although this range was at the bottom of the rental housing market price, it was still beyond their ability to pay up front. Their average yearly income in 2005–2006 was around $12,000, a little more than a quarter of the average yearly income of $40,000 of people ages 35 to 39 reported by the Korea Labor Research Institute in 2007.[8] Their income is insufficient to cover average living expenses (apart from housing costs) in Seoul, which were $1,200 for a single household, given that their monthly housing costs are between $500 and $700 (see the next section for a detailed discussion of lump-sum deposits and monthly fees). In short, my informants belong to the working poor despite their college degrees.

The price of real estate and the use of housing as the major source of household revenue is a product of the particular history of the South Korean capitalist state. Until the crisis in 1997, South Korean banks were under the strict control of the state. The prioritized clients of bank loans were big corporations supported by the South Korean military regimes. In the state-planned economy, the debts of big corporations were considered to be inevitable byproducts of a strategy leading ultimately to profits and the expansion of the national economy, as well as being an unavoidable element of export-centered economic policy (Eun Mee Kim 1997; Woo-Cumings 1999). The military regimes encouraged ordinary people (even schoolchil-dren) to save money in order to reduce the big corporations' burden of debt repayment, but the interest rates people received on their own savings were very low. Getting a loan for personal use, including housing, was almost impossible. Instead, individuals in need of housing were advised to keep a savings account specifically for housing (*chutaek ch'ôngyak yegûm*), which would allow them to bid on new condominiums (*chutaek ch'ôngyak kwôn*) but could not be used for an apartment lease. There were limited housing loan programs (*chutaek tambo taechul*) for ownership but not for tenancy.[9] The only people who had access to credit were the less than 20 percent of the labor force employed as full-time regular workers in big corporations, who could get credit through their employers as part of their benefits. The limited capacity for borrowing money for housing (especially rental housing) from banks meant that usury and personal loans made through the social network flourished.

Many Koreans assume that the national housing bank's savings account to allow bidding rights for the purpose of the purchase of condominiums is a fair process that can make everyone's dream of home ownership come true.[10] This reinforces the presumption that rental housing is a transitional residential form. However, for working poor, including my research participants, rental housing is the only option in the long term and may be how they will have to live permanently. Although working-poor people can bid to purchase a condominium unit if they have a long-term savings account for housing, single-person households are the lowest priority in the bidding process, and the working poor cannot compete for a premium (*p'ûrimiôm*) added to the price of the condominium during the bidding process, because they do not have the lump-sum cash needed. In this structure, anyone without substantial savings has no way of leasing an independent living space.

Most of the young single women I interviewed borrowed money from their families to lease a cheap apartment. Chunhee, who pointed out the different experiences of men and women moving away from home, said that "in order to get your own place, you need to receive seed money (*chongjatton*) from your parents. If you leave without any seed money, even if you have a job, the deposit is too big to pay out of your salary." Some of the women did not pay back the family loan, considering it as money that would have been given to them as a dowry if they had gotten married. Seeing this money as a gift should be understood in the context of Korean social-economic history rather than as a sense of entitlement on the women's part.[11] One interviewee, Sônu, is an exception from the reliance on a family loan for seed money. Her boss gave her a personal loan and let her pay back the principle and interest from her monthly paycheck over a number of years. She saw it as compensation for her loyalty to the faltering small company during the Asian financial crisis.

The family/marriage-centered sexual norm is manifested not only in social and family pressure to marry (and reproduce) but is embedded in Korea's housing loan policies. As already noted, unmarried people under thirty-five years old cannot apply for a bank loan for a yearly lease for housing. Togyông, a single woman in her late thirties working in a low-paying women's organization where her salary is less than $1,000 per month, noticed that her unmarried brother received a bank loan very swiftly, whereas she and her women friends found they were required to have parents or husbands as guarantors in order to apply. Given that the yearly lease is the conventional form of rent in South Korea, being unable to access loans is a critical limitation for the unmarried women I interviewed. Chagyông once mentioned that a debt can also be an asset (*pit to chasan I da*) in the sense that only people who demonstrate capability can get loans. This is congruent to the way in which debt became understood as an asset in the sense of credit or a mortgage in British household economy when financial asset management changed from saving to investment (Langley 2008).

The Ministry of Finance and the Economy and the Ministry of Construction and Transportation control the national housing fund that lends annual lease money (*chônse chagûm*) to individuals in special need, such as newlywed couples and families with children in which the breadwinner makes less than minimum wage, by distributing the money to these individuals through private banks. Officials from these ministries told me in 2006 that only married people or people intending to marry soon (with evidence of a wedding date) are allowed to apply for loans. People who do not intend to marry are not considered to be an "actual demand group" (*silsuyoja*) unless they are more than thirty-five years old and have a record of living alone for several years.[12] These rental housing and banking loan policies discriminate against single women with unstable jobs, because they do not have the money to survive on their own for a few years before applying for the loan.

Private secondary financial institutions (as opposed to banks, which are primary financial institutions) such as venture capital companies, insurance companies, and stock companies, have similar criteria. Haein, who worked in a secondary financial institution in 2005, revealed that most do not provide loans to single women more than thirty-three years old, including divorced women, because they are considered to be an "abnormal" household. She grumbled about the irony of working in a loan business but being unable to apply for a loan herself. Although secondary financial institutions do not state these regulations transparently, these kinds of internal rules are applied without explanation to applicants with the excuse that credit criteria are confidential. As a result, my research participants, such as Togyông, Wony, Tojin, and Yoon, who all tried to get housing loans, said that it was impossible due to the discriminatory regulations that banks and secondary financial institutions imposed upon unmarried women.

Public housing that aims to accommodate the disenfranchised population (*kong'gong imdae chutaek*) does not attend to the particular needs of single women. In 2005, the public housing created for single women (*yôsông chônyong imdae chutaek*: women-only state-leased affordable condominiums) was, for the first time, confined to women less than thirty years old. In addition, priority was given to women working in manufacturing, the accommodation was shared with three or four other women, and there was a curfew.[13] This type of public housing is different from existing public housing in that it has a curfew and does not recognize women's single households as legitimate. Tojin, a single woman in her late thirties who tried to live in this type of women's housing, noted that it was seen as a sojourn for young single women on their way to marriage. As such, it provided surveillance of women's sexuality in the name of protecting their chastity. She said,

> I was once accepted to public housing for single women. But I decided not to go there because I found out I had to live with five other people in a five hundred square foot apartment. That's inhumane! Besides, it's only for women under thirty years old, who are considered to be adolescents rather than adult women. Those places are like private studying rooms for students (toksôsil), with strict regulations for using the place, such as keeping a midnight curfew.

This sexual regulation of single women in public housing is congruent with the widespread chastisement of young women for their sexual morals. Young women engaged in prostitution were criticized by the media, academics, and government policy makers as being morally slack and for engaging in sex work in order to finance "unnecessary" consumption (Cheng 2005; Yi T-h. 1999). The fact that sex work may have been the only source of income for them and/or their family when many breadwinners were laid off was not considered.[14] Housing welfare was not a priority of the Korean state welfare system, despite the great need for it by the working poor and particularly by women and children suffering from domestic violence. For instance, women's shelters for domestic violence, sexual violence, young unwed mothers, and later for homelessness were not expanded, even when stretched beyond their capacities.[15]

Sipûtû, or Shift, is a public long-term rental housing development set up by Seoul City and the public housing company in 2007. It was meant to supply 150,000 units in the following two years, but only seven thousand units had been built by 2009. Shift was ambitiously launched to provide an alternative to home ownership—a decent place to live for the long term. However, housing critics report that Shift is not destined for working-poor people because it is becoming promising real estate for the middle class. My research participants reported that Shift targets middle-class professionals who can afford to pay high utility bills and interest on the bank loan they need to come up with the lease deposit.[16] Bogeumjari Chutaek (nest housing) is a new-millennium plan for mixing ownership and rent for new condominiums. Similar to Shift, it has not kept the promise of unit supply. Another new possibility that some single women attempt (although none of my research participants have) is to bid on a new condominium by using the quota of leftover units open to low-income households. The

opportunity of insufficient sales is rare, and even when it does arise, the
public housing quota requires regular payment before and after purchase,
making it difficult. As in all the other cases, single-person households are
again the lowest priority.

   This frustration of finding housing (either private rental or public) is
closely linked to single women's anxiety about financial insecurity in their
elder years. As a result, many unmarried women would like to emigrate to
North America or Australia/New Zealand. Some of my research participants
attended immigration orientations offered by Canada, Australia, and New
Zealand. However, in most cases, emigration is problematic because of the
women's lack of economic resources or a professional career. Instead, they
have had to settle for traveling or studying English abroad.[17]

   For my research participants, acquiring a dwelling place of their own
demanded perseverance against social norms embedded in banking and public housing loan policy. In order to understand the action of single women's
acquisition of independent living places as resistance to the South Korean
repressive patriarchal state, it is essential to examine the broader political
economy of housing and the lending system, which has been oppressive not
only to women but to working-poor people in general.

The Rental System and the Lump-Sum Cash Market: Sedimented Financialization

Chônse is a yearly or biannual house lease system. The renter deposits a
lump sum (mokkton) representing between 50 and 80 percent of the price
of the apartment at the beginning of the lease, and the landlord returns it
at the end of the lease. It is notable not only that the lump-sum deposit is
transmitted through cash but that it is returned without interest. Although
a recent law has forced landlords to pay a legal interest rate if the deposit
is not returned on time and the tenant files a complaint with the housing
legal system, there is no interest imposed if the deposit is paid back on time
at the end of the lease. For example, if a 300 square foot studio or one-
bedroom apartment in a low-priced area is worth 300 million won (approximately $300,000), it is annually or biannually leased through a lump-sum
security deposit of 200 million won (about $200,000).[18] There can also be
a combination of a yearly lease and monthly rent—requiring, for instance,
a security deposit of 50 million won ($50,000) with a monthly payment of
1 to 2 percent of the rest of the yearly deposit ($150,000), which amounts
to between $1,500 and $3,000 (0.01, or 0.02 × $150,000). A lot of cash
is required up front to begin rental housing in Korea. Because owning a
house is a normalized practice and a common aspiration in South Korea,
many Korean people presume that rental housing is temporary or that it

represents a transitional stage on the way to home ownership.[19] Despite this normative view, it is not necessarily the case for many working-poor people, who lack family resources.

During and after the Asian financial crisis, the monthly payment option was relatively popular for landowners, because they were also affected by mass layoffs and welcomed a higher monthly payment with reduced deposit in order to secure their monthly income. The average security deposit paid by my research participants (when I met them in 2005 and 2006) amounted to around $40,000, with an additional $500 a month paid in rent. At the time, my research participants' income averaged around $1,000 per month. The only way to stick to the monthly payment of $500 was to increase the lump-sum cash deposit. Their housing was in poor condition, as indicated by the low value of their apartments. However, even $40,000 is not easily affordable for people in their thirties or early forties who are patching together an income from irregular work.

It is important to situate the rent system and lending policy in the context of the real estate economy and nature of financial markets in South Korea. The urban real estate market in South Korea is volatile and a major source of both asset accumulation and class polarization in South Korean history (H. B. Shin 2008). Following the Korean War (1950–1953) and the period of military coups and dictatorship (1960–1987), during which there was a rapid change in the economic focus of South Korea, from agricultural to industrial production, there was massive peasant migration to the cities. People moved in particular to Seoul, the capital, which now is home to a quarter of the country's inhabitants, or half, if we consider metropolitan area. As a result of this massive migration, real estate prices skyrocketed in tandem with condominium development in urban areas, rising more than 300 percent in Seoul between 1986 and 2002 (Gelézeau 2007, Hôh 2008, K-Y. Shin 2003).[20] Three moments of rapid increases in real estate prices, those in the late 1970s, late 1980s, and late 1990s, are of particular note. During these moments, housing markets were fully utilized for and combined with the informal cash market, accelerating the polarization of wealth through money capital (Kim Y. 2004). The possession of real estate is currently the most decisive element in determining affluence and class mobility in South Korea.

What is unique in South Korea is that real estate asset transactions— rent as well as purchases—rely on the lump-sum *cash* market because of a scarcely developed formal lending finance sector. A mortgage market was only introduced in 2003 and is usually available only to people with high, regular incomes. The systems of bank housing loans and housing insurance institutions were also undeveloped, limited to a government-run housing fund until recently. As mentioned earlier, previously, the only way to finance the purchase of a house was to invest in a savings program through which one could bid on a condominium unit. In addition, unlike the recently adopted North American style of mortgage, Korean housing bank loans were available only after the ownership of real estate was assured, and the maximum percentage of a loan for a purchased house was lower (70 percent) than for a North American mortgage (90 percent).

For the most part, a legacy from the years of the military dictatorship and development of the state's economic policies was influential for the regulation of bank lending practices. Readers would remember that from 1960 to 1997, accessibility to bank loans was severely limited for individual households as well as for small- to medium-sized companies. The Korean developmental state controlled the banks, supporting the maximization of production on the part of big corporations (chaebôl), to which most loans (90 percent) were directed.[21]

These big Korean corporations are different from the leading companies of the United States and other advanced capitalist nations in the degree to which they have received favors from their government. There are only about ten chaebôl,[22] including Samsung, LG, and Hyundai, and each conglomerate possesses umbrella groups of companies that are reproduced through nepotism and that encompass all kinds of industrial and service commodities, including automobiles, electronics, high-tech commodities, textiles, clothing, bakeries, restaurants, grocery stores, and department stores. More recently, venture capital firms and other secondary financial institutions have also been included in the chaebôl network.[23] Up until the Asian financial crisis, the massive and rapid production of these conglomerates relied on immense credit to make up for the gap between the production and distribution of commodities. In support of the conglomerates, the Korean developmental state pushed banks to offer low interest rates to big corporations by encouraging individual households to save money, not borrow from banks.[24]

Thus, from the perspective of individual households, the informal loan business and rotating credit associations were much more accessible and lucrative (and featured greater options than banks).[25] Despite the fact that the interest rate on informal loans was more than 60 percent per year (compared to the interest on a bank loan, which was less than 20 percent per year), individual households, as well as small- and medium-sized companies, became regular clients in the informal and unregulated money market.[26] This was because South Koreans had to come up with ways in which not only to provide sufficient funds to pay for swelling house prices but to do so using large amounts of cash up front. One way they dealt with this seemingly impossible task was to magnify the informal loan system using creativity and high risk. The chief method that Korean people devised to cope with the need for the large sums of cash required for the purchase of a house was to transform the housing rental system into a credit system involving the payment and return of lump-sum cash, that is, chônse (Dongchul Cho 2006, Nelson 1991, Renaud 1989).

Given that the real estate market has been a hot topic in politics as well as in research (as part of policy-oriented studies on public housing) and that there has been a shared concern over the harsh conditions of urban housing, it is strange to find that research dedicated to the chônse system is still rare.[27] No one knows the origin of the system, not even the economists, urban planners, and sociologists who discuss real estate and housing issues, nor has there been any substantial mainstream political economic analysis of its role in housing and financial markets.[28] Researchers have recommended changing the forms of public housing and developing more relaxed loan policies. These policy suggestions, however, do not challenge the lump-sum deposit system.[29] I assume that this paucity of attention is because the system completely permeates the process of obtaining housing in South Korea and is so embedded in the culture that alternative mechanisms are unimaginable.[30]

My research participants were not exceptions. None of them criticized this agonizing rent system that discriminates against those without access to a large amount of cash and a well-paying job. Rather, they see the difficulty of coming up with the lump sum as their personal or generational failure. For example, Hosôn, the woman who enjoys living by herself but began to doubt her choice after incessant questions from others, told me that she feels ashamed and embarrassed to ask her mother (or sometimes siblings) for money. When I asked whether she thought of it as society's problem, she replied,

> Well, there are a few women in their twenties and thirties who are really frugal and manage to save a lot. But I'm not sure what I'm doing. I just spend money whenever I have it. I have no concept of economy. While I'm very proud of how I'm living, I hate to beg whenever I have urgent matters that require a lot of cash.

Minsô, the woman who managed to achieve a place of her own (after living with her brother) when her parents moved away from Seoul, also noted that her generation is unable to "build their own lives from scratch" (chasusôngga). Her parents' generation overcame an economic depression after the Korean War, using nothing but familial bonding. She compared that for her parents' generation, the meaning of success was much simpler— "eat well and live well" (chal môk ko chal sa nûn kô), a motto that focused primarily on the family unit. Now her generation's criteria of success are based more on individual merit.

The formation of the housing rental system as a credit system anchored by the circulation of lump-sum cash must be understood within the broader context of Korean financial markets, particularly informal financial markets. The chônse system and the informal credit association (kye) operate in parallel—in what Nelson calls a "creative private credit system" (Nelson 2000, 53). Nelson notes that in the early 1990s, when real estate prices were skyrocketing, the interest rate characteristic of both the informal loan market and the monthly rental payment, when combined with chônse, was 2 percent. As a result, the informal loan business (sachae ôp) or usury operation (koridaegûm) in South Korea has been a significance source of credit for individual households, as well as for small- to middle-sized businesses.

In most South Korean households, it is not unusual to have the excruciating experience of or to hear a neighbor or relative complain about money being lost to a rotating credit association (kye) or to an organizer of such an association (kyeju) who ran away with money. The rotating credit association originated as a method of mutual aid or public insurance in the agricultural mode of production more than a thousand years ago in Korea.[31] In the old times, it involved taking turns providing stored rice or other goods to help people in need or in times of crisis. But it was transformed into a solid financial credit association (more in urban than in agricultural areas), probably during the unstable periods of Japanese colonialism and then during the Korean War.[32] It was magnified and readjusted during the period of economic development (under military coup dictatorships), when individual households could get neither bank loans nor a competitive interest rate on their savings.

In general, a modern kye operates by kye organizers (kyeju) pooling, on a monthly basis, a sum of cash from member contributions. The sum of cash is given to one member each month, based on a predetermined rotation mechanism. Some kye associations operate a little differently. For example, a kye by number (sunbôn kye) rotates credit each month in order of a randomly chosen number, and a kye by auction (nakch'al kye) rotates credit by having members bid for their turn.[33] Janelli and Yim's (1988) insightful ethnographic work on rotating credit associations by randomly chosen numbers (sunbôn kye) notes that this was popular at the time of the development of the cash economy at the peak of the Korean developmental regime in the 1980s, corroborating my argument that money capital was prevalent in the Korean informal sector even before the Asian financial crisis and the aggressive launch of formal financial markets in Korea.

Kye became a less common object of media attention after the Asian financial crisis, when credit card debt, false insurance claims, and the fallen price of stocks and bonds were widespread causes of financial distress. However, informal money markets, including kye practices, have not disappeared;

rather, these practices have become more volatile with the liberalization of formal/public financial markets.[34] For example, Choi Chin-sil, a famous actor, committed suicide in September 2008, purportedly due to stress from the rumor that she was a loan shark. The impact of her suicide was significant, because she was adored by Koreans of all ages and genders.[35]

The state has never been able to zero in on rotating credit associations, in spite of several attempts to regulate them (M. Lee 2005; Nelson 2000). One important reason for this is because under-the-table kye practices are profoundly gendered. The primary participants in kye are women household representatives, mostly without a wage income from regular employment.[36] They risk pejorative reputations when their involvement goes wrong and is caught by the government, a risk compounded by the fact that they often deny their husbands' awareness. Because they do not have an official record of making money and their frequent cash transactions are not easily traceable as revenue, the money invested through kye and personal loans is tax free. In short, household assets are primarily accrued through women, and women are known as and expected to be the key figure in mobilizing a family's class through children's education and marriage.[37]

This gendered division of labor between work for wages (undertaken primarily by men) and informal money markets (in which women are the central participants) results from a shortage of women's employment in regular job markets. In particular, women who are part of a normative family household (those consisting of a breadwinning husband and one or more schoolchildren) are responsible for the financial security of the household in connection to one of their primary domestic concerns—managing children's education and early career development. Children's education, in addition to the cost of getting their children married (for both sons and daughters, although the marriage costs for daughters can be more costly to parents) takes a lot of lump-sum cash, to pay for private after-school learning, bribes to teachers and personnel in institutions related to military service and university entrance, and to children's employers (S. J. Park and Abelmman 2004).[38]

Even though it is gendered, modern kye practice is not accessible to all women. It is exclusive to housewives and mothers whose life paths and patterns are linked through their conjugal identity, maternal identity, and in-law identity. The recruitment of kye members is mostly through social networks of family, marriage, home town, and schools in order to minimize liability (by failing to keep money throughout the rotation or by its disappearing outright). Women who distance themselves from marriage and family are a good example of people who are marginalized in this private credit market because of their weak social networks. Even if unmarried women

join some kye through high school or university alumni networks—more
to keep up their contacts than as a source of financial management—they
are sidelined when other members get married and become parents because
of the lack of common interests, as well as stigmatization by newly married
peers of those maintaining a single lifestyle. For instance, my informant
Chagyông stopped being invited places by her social network of college
alumni after she challenged her male colleagues' insults implying she was a
deficient adult. Another informant, Hosôn, gradually withdrew from regular
kin gatherings because of her identity as an unmarried woman.

In spite of these gendered and family/marriage-centered practices that
limit women's locations because of marriage and motherhood, involvement
in informal financial markets in South Korea is prevalent across class. It
involves more than just affluent people, because everyone needs lump-sum
cash for subsistence and social costs. The range of lump-sum cash usage
includes housing (both purchase and rental), education (both formal education and private after-school expenses), weddings (whether hosting or
attending as a guest), and all kinds of gifts for celebration and condolence
(kyôngjosa). The occasions of celebration and condolence that involve cash
gifts include birthday congratulations (especially for babies on their hun-
dredth day and their first birthday and for adults on their sixtieth, sev-
entieth, and eightieth birthdays), anniversaries, exams (university and big
corporation entrance exams as well as professional exams for high officials
above level three [samuguan], prosecutors, judges, lawyers, and diplomats),
graduation, and any outstanding achievement. Although these are evidently
classed issues in that people with more money capital can better participate in money-gift transactions, the way people participate is based on the
principle of reciprocity. For example, Minsô was shocked when her father
retired earlier than expected, motivating her parents to move to the countryside. In leaving his job, her father gave up the reciprocal gifts of money
that he would have received from having given his coworkers money gifts
for their family rituals, such as children's weddings and parent's funerals.[39]
Getting married is the optimal opportunity to garner lump-sum cash, which
is used to compensate parents for the expense of marrying their children
and supports the newlywed household in terms of honeymoon, furniture,
or housing. The cash gift is collected in the wedding hall or church by the
most trusted person (usually a family member) from both the bridegroom's
and bride's families.[40] When these gifts are received, the names of givers
and the amounts of money are both recorded so each family remembers the
minimum amount of money it will be necessary to give in return. This kind
of money gifting is a source of seed money for lump-sum cash that they can
invest through informal credit associations (kye).

Thus, the need for and supply of lump-sum cash is universal and normalized across classes in South Korea, which means people are accustomed to maneuvering for any advantage that will help them create revenue through financial markets: money that makes money (through interest).[41] This is the context in which the Korean rent system is considered lucrative. For the landlord, it is a promising business, because he or she is able to access funds, in the form of the lump-sum deposit, on which to earn interest. Before the crisis, as mentioned above, banks were regulated by the state government, and most landlords (or any person with cash seeking interest-bearing capital or money-making-money) invested their tenants' deposits in informal loan markets or purchased another condominium for a higher return.[42] Tenants' lump-sum deposits have been advantageous not only for middle-class people, who might lease a second house, but for working-class people, who rent out a part of their own house to generate lump-sum cash so they can buy a larger condominium when their children are born or are growing up (Nelson 2000). Gaining a deposit of lump-sum money is a crucial strategy in moving toward the cash purchase of a house or condominium. It is not an exaggeration to say that many middle-class people in Korea have achieved upward mobility from the working class by maneuvering this lease money.[43] There are few disadvantages for the landlord. Even if the landlord does not have the deposit money to return to the tenant at the end of the lease, it is conventionally accepted that the outgoing tenant will be asked to attend a meeting with the landlord and the incoming tenant at a real estate agent's office. At this meeting, the incoming tenant's deposit money is passed on to the outgoing tenant.[44] If the landlord loses the original deposit and cannot find a new tenant, however, and cannot get an informal loan to cover the debt, he or she is at risk of losing the property in order to pay the debt. The anxiety of (not) finding a new tenant on time may be the most significant drawback for a landlord.

Although the exchange value of chônse is high—more than half the purchase value of the property—Korean tenants are inclined to think that paying monthly rent amounts to an outright loss of money, as noted earlier. Tenants whose jobs are unstable and whose incomes are irregular want to increase their lump-sum deposits in order to reduce their monthly payments. This explains why my research participants think it is better to borrow more money for the lump-sum cash deposit when their roommates moved out, as they preferred to pay the chunk of money for their lump sum to paying a monthly rental fee.

The chônse system has been criticized for not being beneficial to tenants. The suggestion has been made that adopting a monthly rental system would be more beneficial for the working poor (Nelson 1991). Although even working-class tenants can make use of the chônse system as a way of mobilizing lump-sum cash and thus attaining a larger living space, I agree with Nelson that it is essential to have more options for people who will likely never own a house. In particular, people whose income and revenue are limited and who have limited social capital in relation to marriage and family are usually unable to come up with the lump sum required to purchase a residence. For them, rental housing should consist of a sustainable form of permanent housing that they can attain with their limited funds. Thus, the government needs to change the policy of rental housing loans by removing the age and marriage priority. Further, it should keep its promise to expand rental loans and provide a significantly increased public rental housing capacity that would not be part of the middle class real estate market but would accommodate people without solid regular incomes. Last, this is connected to the broader concern of globalizing financial practices through the window of Korean context: the literacy of speculating money capital that was already developed before formal financial market was exploded in global scale might have further (negative) implication of how and why money capital (through interest-making in general and in-kind rewards, such as, point cards) became omnipresent in the lives of working poor families and precarious workers as a significant source of survival.

Postcrisis Insecurity and Global Financialization

The longstanding social habit of paying for both small and large purchases with cash up front persists in South Korea. The introduction of credit cards and a mortgage system have had a serious negative impact on working-poor people, even though these measures were implemented with the expectation of providing more opportunity to the working poor. A good example is the fact that since the early 2000s, 16 percent of the working population in South Korea were identified as credit bankrupt and on the blacklist of credit card companies, the loan industry, or employers. This means they were not only incapable of participating in any economic activity but were social pariahs or homeless (for general impact on households, see Kim Sun-yông 2011, Nelson 2006, Seo 2012; for young adults' credit card debt resulting in homelessness, "Young Hope," 2008). At the same time, private lending practices did not diminish, nor did most Korean households seem willing to give up their efforts to minimize payment of any interest. This tendency to use cash for daily as well as big-ticket consumption highlights the significance of interest-bearing capital. People's efforts to reduce obligations to pay interest is based upon the same logic as that involved in maneuvering interest-bearing capital, seeking the maximization of return through informal loan markets as well as through stock and bond markets, secondary financial institutions, and banks. The profusion of mundane transactions undertaken through the use of lump-sum cash undergirds the reliance of Korean people on finance capital, particularly interest-bearing capital, in the construction of Korean capitalism.

Thus, South Korean people have long been accustomed to speculating, which is heralded elsewhere, such as in North America, as a core principle of the neoliberal economy, with the catchphrase "high risk for high return." Although formal financial markets have become more obvious targets of profit making in South Korea since the Asian financial crisis, the expanded scale of speculation through global stock markets do not self-evidently expose how the expansion occurred in part and parcel with the infrastructure of informal financial markets that already existed in parallel to the four decades-long state-planning economy (H-J. Chang 2002; S-W. Cho 2009; Pan 2008), and how the expansion further stratified experiences of different financial classes through the convergence of sedimented and global financializations (Crotty and Lee 2005a; J-h. Jang 2011; K-Y. Shin 2003). People who were marginal both in financial, market-driven asset accumulation and in the labor market (in regard to regular employment), such as my research participants, hardly participated in or benefited from cash transactions in sedimented financialization and stock markets in global financialization. Nevertheless, they were aware of the new financial products, including minus accounts (similar to debit accounts, as I explain later), credit cards, enlarged stock and bond market trades, short-term savings bank or venture capital items with high interest or tax exemptions, and, most of all, insurance products.[45] My research participants were often anxious about their inability to utilize these products after South Korea opened its financial markets to foreign companies in line with the new liberal economic policies. These policies forced local banks, insurance and credit card companies, and health-care providers to create higher-interest financial products and more flexible loans in order to compete with foreign companies. After the banks lost their major clients (big corporations), they sought deposits from and were open to making loans to ordinary Koreans. The subsequent expansion of the financial market (in the formal context) into this smaller scale was unprecedented in South Korea, as credit cards became legitimate (Nelson 2006), small bank loans became possible through debit cards (called a minus account, *mainôs t'ongjang*), and life, education, injury, and health insurance became omnipresent and soon, central, to people's lives.[46]

In addition, numerous types of point cards from franchises rapidly became ubiquitous as a method of saving and making free cash. The point cards' networks include coffee shops (such as Starbucks, Coffee Bean, Seattle Coffee), bakeries (such as Paris Croissant, Paris Baguette, Tous Les Jours, Twosome Places, Dunkin Donuts, Creamy Donuts), and restaurants (such as Chili's, Outback Steakhouse, Kentucky Fried Chicken, Pomodoro, Il Mare).

Whenever I have visited South Korea over the last seven years, people ask me why I don't use point cards. Usually the conversation begins with a cashier asking if I have a point card right before I make a payment. When I say I don't use the cards, they always ask me why not. Even when I explain I do not have time or will not be able to use it for long, most say it would still be useful and effective the next time I visit Korea. They find it odd that I do not make use of the opportunities for free purchases or gifts that are transferred from accumulated points.

This postcrisis financial market has extended the scope and forms of money capital (interest-bearing capital) to every direction and corner, especially through the creation of the pseudomoney system of point cards. Stock markets and official credit loan markets are available to people who have more established assets; the point card system appeals to children, students, and young adults without much disposable income. In this way, the logic of interest-bearing capital, or the myth of getting free money through interest or through collecting points and mileage, as the crux of financial capitalism seeds its vast infrastructure from the bottom.[47] However, the people who start with more money always have the foundation to make more money, and this phenomenon is justified rather than challenged by the small-scale practices in building assets through utilizing financial products such as point cards.[48]

The use of these kinds of financial products and options, labeled "financial know-how" (chaet'ekû), became inevitable for ordinary people if they were to have socioeconomic security. Individuals could no longer expect lifelong employment, and the newly launched national pension plan was not trusted because of the state bureaucracy's reputation for corruption and mismanagement. My research participants were anxious about whether they were taking proper advantage of these techniques of property growth. Most considered personal and private financial investments to be necessary to ensure their future security. Regardless of affordability, they seemed to think that these techniques were available to everyone, depending only on their individual skills in information management. If they did not possess this set of skills, they tended to consider it to be their own fault, as Wony articulated in the quote that starts this chapter. And Hosôn said:

> I don't have much to tell you if we talk about my life plan. I'm not ready at all. So far, I have just liked the way I lived, enjoying it as it is. I like meeting people who have a critical perspective similar to mine, especially meeting them over a drink in the evening. I just feel happy. My relatives lecture me about whether enjoying life in the here and now will be good forever. Then I realized that I have been living without a plan (taechaek i ôpsôtta). [smile] I don't have a plan for next year, not to mention what to do when I get

old (*nohu taechaek*). I'm really weak in the face of the questions about "when I get old" (*nohu*).

When I asked her about the national pension as a possible solution, Hosôn replied:

> I don't think the national pension would be a solution for securing my elderly years (nohu taechaek). They have been saying that the pension money will be drained by the time I receive a pension. Even though some pension money will be left for me, it will not be sufficient to meet the living standard for me to enjoy any cultural activities such as watching a movie. I think it would be a bit of pocket money for public transportation (*ch'abi chôngdo*). [smile] That would not be a solution for my elderly years.

Hosôn's concern about financial insecurity in her elderly years and her negative opinion about the national pension is echoed by many other research participants. Haein, the woman working in a secondary financial institution, actively sought to secure her elderly years by entering a more risky job market and setting up several private insurance and pension accounts in preparation for her retirement. Haein noted:

> Living a single life will require more money for being sick when you get old because no one is taking care of you. *That's why I am trying to find and move to a high-risk, high-paying job*, like that of a real estate auction agent, because there is no lifelong secure job available anyway. *Since I know I don't trust the national pension system, I have several private insurance plans.* Unless single women can afford to emigrate to North America, we don't have any prospects here. So we need more vigilant preparation for maximum profit making; we need to seek useful information and enhance ourselves to adapt to the information we find. (italics added)

When I asked Minsô whether she had joined the national pension plan, she was adamant that "I cannot trust the national pension system. The contribution criteria are absurd. My friend's family has five unmarried daughters and her father did not have a stable job, but the family had to pay two *chôn man won* (approximately $20,000) per year. I was forced to pay even though I didn't have a job." Minsô added:

> I am most concerned about when I get older (*nohu kôkjjông*) as an unmarried woman. It is a serious problem to figure out how I will

feed myself then. When the national economy crashed [during the crisis] and all the public responsibilities rested on the shoulders of individuals, I came to think of private insurance as the only solution. Somebody lured me into it, saying it would be cheaper if I began early. So when I was around twenty-seven, I bought life insurance (*chongsin pohôm*) and two health insurance policies that specialize in cancer (*am pohôm*) and women's diseases (*puinbyông*). I bought them through a staff member of the women's organization I was affiliated with, who was also an insurance company agent. You know, NGO workers can't make a living with their salary. I used her as my insurance agent to kind of help out another woman and the women's movement, but I don't feel good about the fact that my insurance products are all from big conglomerates.

Chisu explained why people don't trust the national pension plan. She said:

People are pessimistic about what the government can do for us. The media report that the fund will be drained by 2040. I don't trust that taxes and the pension will be distributed with regard for the social good, especially to poor people.[49] Rather, I think the money will be used for government workers' retirement pensions, given the history of corruption. It actually affects everyone, whether people have unstable or stable jobs. Everyone is obsessed with finding solutions for their elderly years. If the Korean state welfare system were well established, I wouldn't have to worry about whether I would get anything after years of taxes and pensions. People wouldn't feel they had wasted their money and their work. That is why people are thinking of tax fraud all the time. The Korean welfare system displaces government responsibility onto individuals' shoulders. So I started a private pension through insurance companies. If I put in 500,000 won ($500) every month for seven years, I heard I can get about 300,000 won ($300) a month after I'm sixty years old, until I die.

Two unmarried women friends of Chisu were present at the interview. One friend encouraged Chisu to buy a condominium, not as a place to live but as an asset. She provided an alternative suggestion to Chisu's private pension plan:

Hey, we don't know when we'll die. What's the use of receiving 300,000 won ($300) per month after turning sixty years old? You have to have a bolder investment and financial technique. Instead of the [private] pension plan, buy a condominium. Then you can rent out the condominium and enjoy your life with either [interests born from] the lump-sum cash deposit [from yearly rent] or monthly cash income.

This conversation is a vivid example of how postcrisis financial insecurity amplifies the precrisis financial habit of small-scale speculation and lump-sum cash transactions as the best way to accumulate assets and battle the anxiety of present and future insecurity.

In short, the South Korean lease system is a device consisting of the informal loan of lump-sum cash in place of a system in which landlords charge only rent. Even though the renter does not get interest for lending the money to the landlord, the landlord gets an opportunity to receive a large cash loan and invest it for interest elsewhere, with a low amount of risk. In tandem with the rise of new financial techniques that became ubiquitous in people's daily lives after the Asian financial crisis, the significance of Korean rental housing, the crux of the long-standing speculation tool, was magnified. This is where I see sedimented and global financialization merging in Korean neoliberalism.

What constitutes global financialization in South Korea is the introduction of additional opportunities to maneuver interest-bearing capital, such as credit cards, mortgages, private insurance and pensions, and high-rate saving programs, all of which emerged in the liberalized *formal* financial market following the Asian financial crisis. As evidence of the emergence of finance capital in which industrial capitalists and financial markets merge for the maximization of profits, economists report that big conglomerates owned a significant portion of nonbank financial institutions (NBFI) during the crisis (C. H. Lee, Lee, and Lee 2002). NBFIs are a major channel for individuals such as landlords who receive substantive deposits from chônse, participants in rotating credit, and even usurers, because of their savings or stock options. This kind of global financialization in South Korea is evident, in much more humble ways, in the experiences of my research participants. Given the prevalent social contexts of relying on lump-sum, cash-based transactions and informal financial capital accumulation through usury, kye, and the unique housing rental system, chônse, the predominant theories related to the emergence of the modern Korean economy through chaebôl-led industrial capitalism do not allow us a complete understanding of Korean capitalism, especially in regard to household economy.

Marx predicted the disappearance of informal loan businesses along with the rise of industrial capital because of the need for the centralization of circulation and accumulation to render them more effective (pushing private lenders into institutionalized banks and, later, into the official finance capital system). Yet Korean informal loan and credit markets never faced ruin—before, during, or after the peak of the industrial capital regime. Thus, in Korea, it appears that informal financial capital, especially the rotating credit system, may have been a vital component of capital accumulation during the ascendance of industrial capital rather than fading away under the institutionalization of finance capital. I argue, based on my examination of the Korean case, that in the arena of housing finance, not just the purchase but, uniquely, the rental system is a core element of accumulating interest-bearing capital that did not necessarily exempt working-class people from participation in the capitalist accumulation process. More important, generalizing finance capital simply as fictitious does not work in understanding that both wages and the maneuvering of lump-sum cash have been significant modes of revenue generation that have crossed class lines in the Korean context.

Even in terms of the big picture of the history of Korean capitalism (its accumulation process and crisis), known as the "Miracle on the Han River," and the crisis of state-chaebôl–led economic development, none of this would have been possible without the accompaniment of strong financial markets (informal loan businesses, such as kye or various degrees of usury [sachae and kûn son], which preceded the surge of the stock market). Further, the housing boom was a far earlier instrument for utilizing (interest-bearing or fictitious) capital accumulation; global capital only became prevalent through liberal economic policy. The context of the Korean housing-finance market connection might appear similar to that of North American and European nations currently afflicted by the collapsing housing market and financial markets (Panitch and Gindin 2008). However, the sequence that occurred in the United States—speculation in the housing market by a bank system that led the faltering of housing and (formal) financial markets—is different from the sequence in Korea, where speculation in the housing (and rental) market through household management, constituted crucially of informal financial markets, magnified the expansion of formal financial markets by sustaining the national economy during the Asian financial crisis rather than leading the collapse of the national economy. This comparison is not to support the Wall Street bankers' or anyone's advocacy of speculation as a reliable method of capitalist accumulation but to challenge the tempting generalization that financialization and financial markets rely primarily on the path of U.S. capitalist history.

In sum, I have discussed five clusters of structural constraints for unmarried women's housing and financial security. First, the post–Korean War economy developed a unique financial market that uses lump-sum cash and its interest as the primary method and source of asset accumulation for individual households. Second, the prevalent practice of using rental housing (chônse) is a crucial chain in the circulation of lump-sum cash. Third, there are limited options for financial products and loan opportunities that cater to the needs of the rental housing process, with complicated requirements and a bureaucratic evaluation procedure. Fourth, financial law and bank ordinances naturalized the precedence of married couples and normative households by including regular employment and age regulations in the requirements for applying for loans, especially for rental housing. Fifth, women in general, and particularly young single women, have been unable to provide a regular employment record, a required condition for the loan application. The first three contexts affect all economically disenfranchised people. The fourth context impinges on single people (of all genders) who are not old enough and who do not have proof of living by themselves before applying for a housing loan. The fifth context is crucial to show that there is a gender slippage in the housing needs of financially marginalized groups, such as single women who want to live by themselves or with nonfamily members. Although a heterosexual couple in a common-law relationship would be affected by the fourth context, in that case, the housing problem could be resolved through the resources of the man in the relationship, who is more likely to be eligible than the woman to apply for a rental loan or any other credit through his employment. Single women, a same-sex couple of women, or a household of people not in a familial or sexual relationship are most negatively influenced, especially when those living units consist only of young women who have not or cannot establish their careers in any regular job market.

Within this context of the housing and financial insecurities of unmarried women, the next chapter considers the affective realm of life in the postdemocratized liberal regime that highlights "enjoyment" as a new governing rule of social and individual lives.

CHAPTER 3

Between Flexible Labor and a Flexible Lifestyle

·•·———·•·

A strange delusion possesses the working classes of the nations where capitalist civilization holds its sway. This delusion drags in its train the individual and social woes which for two centuries have tortured sad humanity. This delusion is *the love of work, the furious passion for work, pushed even to the exhaustion of the vital force of the individual and his progeny.* Instead of opposing this mental aberration, the priests, the economists and the moralists have cast a sacred halo over work. Blind and finite men, they have wished to be wiser than their God; weak and contemptible men, they have presumed to rehabilitate what their God had cursed. I, who do not profess to be a Christian, an economist or a moralist, I appeal from their judgment to that of their God; from the preachings of their religious, economics or free thought ethics, to the frightful consequences of work in capitalist society.

—Paul Lafargue, *The Right to Be Lazy* (italics added)

Chagyông, who defied her male colleagues' labeling her as a "deficient" adult because she was unmarried, introduced me to Paul Lafargue's *The Right to Be Lazy* (1907), translated into Korean in 2005. She said the book was popular among her leftist circle of friends and colleagues. She was won over by Lafargue's criticism of the fetishism of the work ethic as an instrument of capitalism. Lafargue argued in the late nineteenth century that in order to change the capitalist world, we should fight for the right to be lazy. Chagyông said "the right to be lazy" was her catchphrase after she read it.

Similarly, the other single women I interviewed underlined enjoyment as a guiding principle. They actively sought a laid-back attitude and exposure to various leisure and cosmopolitan experiences as a way of compensating for an inflexible or stressful life. At the same time, they were highly critical of the neoliberal labor market demand for a more elastic market and the resulting increase in irregular jobs. They recognized that the spatially mobile and deregulated job market brought insecurity to their jobs, housing, and retirement years. Was it a contradiction for them to pursue a flexible lifestyle and at the same time criticize flexible labor? If flexible labor caused them pain, how is it that a flexible lifestyle was perceived as happiness? In other words, how does the liberal ethos of pursuing individual freedom depart from and merge with the neoliberal logic of "plasticizing" individuals to fit into unstable job markets? Did my research participants recognize this as a paradox? How can we make sense of these seemingly incompatible positions?

As a way of answering these questions, I address affect as a key notion and terrain for understanding the way in which the *desires* of these single women to live personally enjoyable lives were shaped by the neoliberalization process. By affect, I mean unconscious emotions rather than feelings channeled through the subject's awareness. These unconscious emotions have an influential power to act and motivate interactions (affecting and being affected). On the one hand, I do not disagree with the perspective that affect and emotion can be interchangeable, in that emotion is a potent source of power for human action and history, no less than reason, and it is easily diffused and contagious on a mass scale, particularly in the case of nationalistic zeal and anger (Ahmed 2004). At the same time, the notion of affect provides a useful tool with which to describe layers of emotion that cannot be explained as cognitive feeling in the realm of human agency yet that powerfully influence the production of ironical desires, discourses, and realities (Ducey 2007; Massumi 2002; Navaro-Yashin 2009).

Massumi (2002) demonstrates the impact of affect in political and financial-economic events in which the impression of someone's confidence and interpersonal intensity is processed more rapidly than logical reasoning and can lead to inexplicable consequences. An example in the political sector is the reelection of Ronald Reagan despite his often incoherent speech and faltering health. Massumi emphasizes that it was the visual image of Reagan's twitch and his overweening confidence that affected audiences to be sympathetic beyond their reasoning process and allowed them to imagine meaning and fulfillment. Massumi notes, "That is why Reagan could be so many things to so many people; that is why the majority of the electorate could disagree with him on major issues but still vote for him" (p. 41). In the financial-economic context, Massumi shows how a stock market commentator's illogical inference (connecting stock market dips to the loss of confidence in Clinton's health-care initiative) is predicated upon the assumption that stock markets are more rapidly influenced by affective fluctuation than by economic calculation. He says,

> The ability of affect to produce an economic effect more swiftly and surely than economics itself means that affect is a real condition, an intrinsic variable of the late capitalist system, as infrastructural as a factor. Actually, it is beyond infrastructural, it is everywhere, in effect. (Massumi 2002, 45)

Affect is very useful in understanding my research participants' paradoxes: in this chapter, analyzing the coexistence of a desire for a flexible life and a critique of flexible labor and the parallel discourses of the enjoying subject and the planning/entrepreneurial subject and, in chapter 4, examining criticism of post-revolutionary inertia and reinterpreting the appearance of dormancy as a self-suspension. In a sense, the notion of affect helps us sharpen the Foucauldian concept of "technologies of the self." As already noted, research participants' concerns about their lack of financial techniques is key to understanding the neoliberal production of subjectivities (or technologies of the self) in terms of the way in which care for the self merges with the search for financial security and entrepreneurship. In this context, affect is a useful, if not enhanced, device with which to conjure up the unnamed domains—feeling that unpredictably influences politics, public sentiments, and stock markets—to complement the notions of technologies of the self and social ethos.[1] Foucault, for example, notes the significance of "hidden feeling" and "movement of the soul," yet he does not focus on articulating what these are.[2]

Further, Slavoj Žižek's concept of enjoyment (*jouissance*), adapted from Lacan, is useful for understanding how the pursuit and management of flexible time and space, with the aim of enjoying our lives and our work, helps to consolidate capitalism. Korean young adults in the post-revolutionary moment, jostled by national and global financial crises, are the necessary fluid surplus population—individuals who, in Žižek's explanation, embody and are embedded in the discourses and practices of "self-sufficiency." Žižek understands enjoyment to be a political factor because "enjoyment is what fixes the subject in its place." He points out that "differing economies of enjoyment—capitalist, socialist, nationalist, racist, sexist—can and do coexist" (Dean 2006, 8–17).[3] As noted, most of the research participants became involved in leftist movements in their college years in the late 1980s and early 1990s and went through the changes in identification immanent in the shift away from radical socialist movements to new, predominantly liberal, social movements. They distanced themselves from militant, male-centered, leftist organizations once they graduated; they became affiliated with women's movements without losing their focus on the working class. In particular, these leftist women commonly said that they had achieved liberal "personhood" (in the feminist consciousness-raising sense) in the course of surviving the leftist student movement, which was notorious for its dogmatic and masculinity-centered culture.[4] They worked at part-time minimum wage jobs not only because of the structural discrimination against women and former student activists but because they sought both jobs and lifestyles that they could enjoy. This is parallel to their preference for living in single households in low-quality dwellings rather than conforming to social norms by living with their parents and the pressure to get married. In short, they were ideologically left and socially liberal in comparison with the ideologically left and socially conservative stance of their former masculinist student activism or the ideologically right and socially liberal position of the current neoliberal regime.

Leftist Trajectories and the Cost of Flexible Labor

The details of the lives of three unmarried women, Chagyông, Tojin, and Sônu, demonstrate the genealogy of their student activism and their irregular employment throughout the Asian financial crisis. It is important to note that these women are not unique. Although they may have a more finely developed consciousness of gendered socialization than some of their less-politicized peers, their experience of being both leftist and liberal is widespread among the large number of former student activists and leftist intellectuals in South Korea. Chagyông, Tojin, and Sônu came from different provinces of South Korea, and each went to a different nonelite university. They also came from different sectors of the leftist student movement. Chagyông and Sônu were influenced by older siblings who had been active in the 1980s student movement, and themselves became involved in the early 1990s.[5] Tojin attended boarding school, but on entering college, she immediately became involved in a radical student movement and became one of the "dogmatic" leaders. All of the women's parents were educated up to primary or secondary school and either urban working poor or peasants, so their understanding of economic disparity came from firsthand experience. The women all entered the job market right after graduation rather than remaining full-time leftist activists. When I interviewed them in 2005 and 2007, Chagyông had for a decade been a contract-job teacher in a private after-school institute (*hakwon kangsa*) for junior high school students, Sônu had been a low-income freelance English translator and tutor (*arûbaitû*) for a few years after vacillating between being a stable office worker and a traveler, and Tojin was transitioning from a seven-year job in a major women's movement organization to a job as a temporary project manager for a local cultural festival. All of them were in their late thirties. It had been on average a decade that they had lived by themselves.

SÔNU

By the time she graduated, Sônu was fed up with the dogmatism of student activism, and she cut herself off from her alumni group. This was significant, because her fellow students were a key social and political economic network, which is the primary channel in South Korea for career advancement, marriage, success in elections, and profitable participation in private loan or rotating credit practices. Her group was predominantly influenced by the National Liberation (NL) sector, which focused on reunification with North Korea and considered *chuche sasang* (sovereignty ideology), as elaborated by Kim Il Sung (the former head of North Korea), to be the primary text of leftist revolution. The other main sector, the People's Democracy (PD), focused on class revolution and labor emancipation based on the texts of Marx and Lenin. Although both leftist sectors were severely oppressed by the anticommunist military regimes of South Korea, NL student activists were detested and persecuted to a particularly extreme degree by the South Korean military government in the context of the Cold War division and competition with North Korea. Sônu said the NL was more socially conservative and militant than the PD, and its organization was hierarchical and secretive. This description was corroborated by other women from an NL background, such as Tojin and Nani.

Sônu was covertly approached by a senior, a cell leader,[6] and she bonded with the senior and another junior colleague as a cell unit. Her trust of the cell leader was broken when she and her junior colleague discovered that the senior was operating several cells at the same time and that the devotion among their cell members was contrived. Sônu felt alienated from the junior colleague as well when she noticed that her colleague was just as dogmatic and instrumental in her thinking as the senior. Sônu's part in the division of labor (that is, the work she did as a member of a cell) was care work—building intimacy with new students by nurturing and taking care of them as if they were her younger siblings—a role her cell colleague despised, preferring to connect with "the brains" of the leftist movement. These experiences made Sônu lose her passion for the movement, and she moved on to her own career after graduation.

Sônu worked as a white-collar worker in a small chemical company for seven years. Her wages barely allowed her to make ends meet, but she lived frugally and saved money for travel to Mexico and Australia. Travel became her passion. The chemical company lent her money to rent an apartment when she decided to move out of her sister's place and allowed her to pay back the loan from her paycheck. She took leave from her job for a year in order to take care of her mother, who was dying and needed full-time care. When she returned to the company, the job felt routine and unchallenging. She found a new job in a small computer company, but still the routinized white-collar work did not interest her. She quit the second job, even though it was during the peak of the Asian financial crisis and a time of mass lay-offs and high unemployment. She was confident of her ability to make a living as an English translator, regardless of the national crisis. However, her livelihood became much less secure, because she did not have a translator's certificate, and tutoring jobs were scarce because she was competing with recent college graduates for fewer job opportunities. Sônu continued to seek a "freer," more enjoyable lifestyle through freelance translation and travel, but she made a precarious working-class income while her savings from former jobs were sapped.

TOJIN

Like Sônu, Tojin came from the national liberation sector in the leftist student movement, but Tojin was loyal to the movement as a leader of her college branch. The leftist movement in Seoul tended to prioritize the worker-intellectual alliance over the peasant-intellectual alliance, but Tojin's college was located in the countryside close to Kwangju, the city of leftist martyrdom. Her group worked closely with the local peasant movement organization.

Tojin's deep involvement in the peasant movement made her very aware of the left's discrimination against women. She realized that the peasant movement mistreated women members. When a woman student activist, a friend of Tojin, was sexually assaulted by a peasant man who was involved in the local movement, men student activists from her university did not address it for fear of breaking the alliance between the peasants and students. As a result, Tojin left for Seoul to look for a new base of activism within the women's movement. She painfully reflected that she had not been so different from her sexist male colleagues, because even as a woman, she had been insensitive to gender and to social issues other than class and reunification. In fact, she sometimes accused herself of being myôngye namsông, an honorary man.

Tojin became active in women's organizations after she moved to Seoul in 1999. She noted that there were many more women's networks and women's social movements—more highly developed radical feminism, in particular—in Seoul than in other areas.[7] Working in a major women's organization was not just enlightening to her as a (gendered) individual but also allowed her to see the process of subsumption on the part of NGOs to state neoliberal welfare policies during the Asian financial crisis. According to Tojin, NGOs with socialist and antistate movement backgrounds began participating in the various state "partnership" programs.[8] However, after receiving state subsidies to implement social programs as well as reporting to and being audited by the government, many small NGOs, despite barely paying their workers the minimum wage, could not get out of a tight chain of financial need.

After working for free for several months, Tojin's first paid job in the women's organization was actually a position in the public works program that was created to support "good" NGOs and NPOs. Her initial wage through the government subsidy was less than $400 per month. Even after she became a manager in the organization in 2005, her monthly wage was less than $1,000. She quit the job in 2005, partially because of the difficulty of living on such a low income in Seoul and partially because she did not think that the women's movement should be "playing a game" with the state. She had a temporary job as a project manager in a local street festival when I met her again in June 2006. She said it was not a "political" space, but she enjoyed the job and the relative freedom it gave her, and the pay was better. She began a peace movement group with other leftists and feminist activists, inspired by Kim Sôn-il. Kim was a South Korean who worked as a translator in Iraq. He was beheaded in June 2004 by Iraqi revolutionary soldiers after the Korean government agreed to support the U.S. military presence in Iraq.[9]

CHAGYÔNG

Chagyông was introduced in chapter 1. She was one of the most economically stable of the women I interviewed. This is in part because her job was relatively secure due to her reputation and accumulated experience in the private after-school job market (despite contract job) and in part because she inherited a small permanent-lease, public housing apartment for low-income people (kong'gong imdae chutaek) from her mother. Although she has siblings, she inherited the apartment because she lived with her late mother and supported her until she died. Chagyông did not describe her student activism, but she revealed that she connected with her former activist colleagues at occasional reunions. The meetings were not without incident, as we have seen.

Chagyông said she had often lost her temper when meeting with her former activist colleagues, many of whom were married to each other. She noted that although married women colleagues rarely discriminated against unmarried members, married men in the circle felt superior to the single ones, both in terms of hierarchy and personal integrity. When arguments were stoked by the provocations of male colleagues—infantilizing her or labeling her as a defective person—she made remarks to make the men feel bad by noting their inability to support their families, which was a big trigger for them. Many male activists had difficulties either because they did not concentrate on their studies during their college years or because employers were unwilling to hire them for political reasons. Her female colleagues also became uneasy with Chagyông. What struck me in hearing her stories was that she continued to see her former colleagues in spite of the blunt confrontations and emotional costs. Her identification as a leftist intellectual and her desire to sustain a connection with her former colleagues was strong. She said that she was pleased when she noticed that her male colleagues had started to be more cautious in their interactions with her.

Chagyông's defiance of her male colleagues' authority is not just a result of her belief in gender equality. It is also a consequence of her desire to control her own time and space and ability to enjoy life. She is the one who pointed me in the direction of The Right to Be Lazy.

"The Right to Be Lazy" and the Joy of a Flexible Life: Travel and the Media

Seeking and achieving one's own place to live, even in a humble rental apartment, is a basic requirement but, at the same time, both financially and socially, the most costly realization of the affective regime of enjoyment. For my research participants, personal exploration would not have been possible without the Korean liberalization of the early 1990s, including the explosive exposure to foreign media and the new freedom of travel. One thing that commonly popped up was my research participants' expressed desire to live or travel abroad—whether because of their frustration with housing and credit-loans, the confining and intrusive social script of marriage and sexual morals, their curiosity, or all three.[10]

Sônu voluntarily quit her job during the Asian financial crisis for a freer life and developed her passion for travel abroad. Chunhee, who ran away from her parents' home because of their controlling behavior and a strict curfew, experienced a few months in Canada to learn English with the full support of her parents. Togyông, who worked in a women's organization at a low wage, still traveled extensively—to six countries in Europe and North America— using most of her savings. Although not all unmarried women went abroad, most wanted to. We can recall Haein's narrative about the good prospects for unmarried women who can afford to immigrate to North America, in contrast to the women like herself left in South Korea. Sojông referred to her sister's backpacking trip to Europe as a sign of her self-confidence, in contrast to herself, who faced more insecure employment—but she also affirmed her dream of studying abroad.[11] To quote her narrative again:

> People like me who graduated in the middle of the crisis don't have any prospects of getting a stable job. But still, there is peer pressure to be successful, cool women in terms of not only having good jobs but of being stylish. I think this emphasis on style and appearance is influenced by *Sex and the City*. It is a matter of whether you are good at self-management. If you are not pretty, it is not just a disadvantage but a sign of being a loser and unable to manage yourself.

She added:

> *Sex and the City* is far more popular than other dramas. Aside from the characters' compulsion to get married, women in their twenties and thirties living alone in Seoul tend to think of protagonists from *Sex and the City* as their models for a stylish and individualistic life.

Of the many films and TV dramas the women were exposed to, including *Bridget Jones's Diary*, *Will and Grace*, *Queer as Folk*, *Ally McBeal*, *Grey's Anatomy*, *CSI*, and *L Word*, *Sex and the City* was the one most often mentioned by my research participants.

Domestic TV programs about unmarried women's lives have also flourished. They include drama and reality TV shows and films and are either heavily fixated on marriage—focusing on, for example, strategic preparations to get married to "nice guys" or funny characterizations of single women's daily lives as being desperate and miserable—or depict a single woman's successful career and independent lifestyle. The many Korean TV dramas centered on single woman characters over the last decade include *Toksin ch'ônha* (Single's World, 2006), *Kyôlhon hago sipûn yôja* (Women Wanting to Get Married, 2004), and *Oldû misû daiôri* (Old Miss Diary, 2004–2005), all of which take after *Sex and the City* and *Bridget Jones's Diary*. In addition, *On Style*, a TV program targeting young women in their twenties and thirties with an interest in fashion, is a reality TV show with the theme of "contrasexuals"—single urban professional women with a liberal lifestyle.[12] A special documentary, *Sing'gûl ira to kwaench'an a* (It Is Fine for a Woman to Be Single),[13] sponsored by Munhwa Broadcasting Company (MBC) in partnership with a Japanese broadcasting company, also fit the polarized representation of single women as either waiting to be married or extremely successful and independent. It actually merges the two images into one: although it focuses on career women with stable jobs who own their own homes, its main theme is that these women *want* to get married but have a difficult time balancing their careers and dating.

Further, mass media discourses on "soybean women" or the "golden miss," especially in online blogs and reality TV shows, demonstrate the polarization of the image of young unmarried women.[14] "Soybean women" (*toenjang nyô*) is a hostile term for young unmarried women who consume expensive commodities by depending on parents or boyfriends. They aspire to be part of a high-end cosmopolitan culture by, for example, drinking Starbucks coffee and seeking (fake) famous brands. "Golden miss" (*koldû misû*), on the other hand, is a label for single women who are seen to be too successful and affluent to find a partner. The golden miss is understood to be deserving of taking pleasure in high-end consumption because of her extraordinary personal capabilities. This image is predicated upon an assumption that unmarried women are women who are waiting to be married (mihon).

Given that my research participants identify not with the designation of "not yet married" (mihon) but with the new notion of "unassociated with marriage" (pihon) and that these domestic TV shows typify independent single women as upper middle or upper class women, my research participants do not identify with these programs. Nevertheless, most of my research participants who watch TV adore the foreign dramas, despite the distance from their reality. The foreign dramas seem to offer sources of inspiration for travel abroad and ways to find freedom and enjoyment in life. For instance, as an attempt to immerse themselves in a low-cost cosmopolitan experience, some of my research participants have participated in inexpensive social dance groups (including swing and salsa) run by a progressive women's personal network. They want to explore "bodily pleasures," to liberate themselves from the rigid bodily habits and dogmatic fashion codes of the student activists and intellectuals they once were.

To Chagyông, her pleasure from after-work gatherings, leisure (swimming, aerobic workouts, hiking), and hobbies (swing dance, salsa, wearing costumes) is a sign that she has her own life and that she is liberated as an individual. This is very different from the lives of many of her former activist colleagues who took the route of a normative life, such as with marriage, family, and competition for the education of their children. For all the unmarried women I interviewed, including Chagyông, Tojin, and Sônu, their independent lifestyle is a crucial marker of who they are: ideologically left and socially liberal. It is something they are consciously aware of and put their energy into out of their own desire and motivation (specifically, they can and want to enjoy life) rather than something they think they "should" do.

It is notable that sexual pleasure was hardly mentioned by my research participants, even when I asked them about it directly. This is somewhat surprising, considering the popularity of *Sex and the City* and other foreign

TV dramas, as already mentioned. The sexual affairs of married couples was a key theme of domestic films such as *Sing'gŭljŭ* (Singles, 2003), *Kyŏlhon ŭn mich'in chisi ta* (Marriage Is Insane, 2000), and *Param nan kajok* (Family in Affairs, 2003), as well as TV dramas such as *Pulkkot* (Flare, 2000). My research participants clarified that the sex talk in foreign dramas was not applicable in the Korean context and was rarely a subject of their personal conversations, even with close friends. One interviewee commented that *Pulkkot* (Flare) mirrored the crisis of middle-aged men during the Asian financial crisis whose work stress and risk of being laid off went up and who had no other channel for pleasure than sexual pleasure outside of marriage. Another interviewee spoke highly of the drama's romantic aspect but not its treatment of sexual desire.

The pursuit of a laid-back and enjoyable lifestyle or of individuality is not a trait limited to my research participants. It is a new attribute in South Korea because many citizens are uncertain about the benefits of industrial capitalism and ponder the benefits of going back to a pastoral or farming life in the country as a remedy to high-speed urban industrialization.[15] In addition, citizens are preparing themselves and future generations to fit into post-Fordist capitalist production, which requires increased individualization to provide the flexible labor that can adapt to the anomalous markets of information, communication, and service.

Members of South Korean society in their twenties to early forties, who are less driven to achieve socioeconomic upward mobility than members of their parents' postwar, poverty-stricken generation and who have fewer opportunities in the stable job markets, are reclaiming the label of "good for nothing" (paeksu) derogatorily attached to underemployed young adults.[16] It is part of a new creative lifestyle that includes a fuzzy boundary between work and leisure (resulting in part-time/contract work as a favorable "option"—although it is sometimes the only option) and a strong sense of one's uniqueness and self-sufficiency. Pak Chu-yŏng's *Paeksu saenghwal paeksŏ* (Everything about a Good-for-Nothing), a novel that won a prestigious literary competition (*Onŭl ŭi chag'ga sang* [Today's Writer]) in 2006, is a story about a woman who has been a fanatical reader since she was young and continues to be so after graduating from university. She never bothers to look for a job. Reading is her passion in life and her way of communicating with the world as much as it is an instrument to avoid exposure to the world. She does not care about career development and she does not mind working as a gas station attendant when she needs to, when her basic subsistence is threatened. The narrator feels no shame or guilt that she is not using her college degree. Rather, she and two friends (Ch'ae-rin and Yu-hŭi) are boldly proud of self-centeredness as a marker of their new generation. The novel ends in this way:

Ch'ae-rin [whose extramarital affairs were her only joy in life] does not love for someone else. Nor does she love for the sake of love. She loves only for herself, as her life is solely hers. Yu-hûi [smart but unpredictable, who has recently become a writer] does not write stories for others. Nor does she write stories for the sake of literature. She writes only for herself, as her life is solely hers. And I read books only for myself. (p. 323, my translation)

Flexible Life and Enjoyment

The new market of the post-Fordist economy and the global financialization in the South Korean context, both of which we associate with neoliberalism, circulate particular commodities, information, and affects that do not fit into the mass production system characteristic of the Fordist economy. Everything about the individual is easily valorized and appropriated in the technologies of self of neoliberal human capital, resulting in the rapid spread of capricious commodities (E. Kim 2012; Seo 2009; Song 2009b). "Compulsiveness with self-development" (chagi kyebal kangbakchûng) or distress at not being able to cope with social trends is depicted daily in the newspapers as a pathological symptom.[17] New commodities recommended to help manage these anxieties include expensive daily schedulers and best-selling self-help books. Many American and Japanese self-help books on how to be successful have been published in Korea and have been best sellers since the crisis. Saisho Hiroshi's Morning-Style Person (Ach'im hyông in'gan, 2003), Robert Kiyosaki's Rich Dad Poor Dad (Puja appa kanan han appa, 2000), Stephen Covey's The Seven Habits of Highly Effective People (Sôngkong ha nûn saram tûl ûi ilgopkaji sûpkwan, 2004), Joachim de Posada and Ellen Singer's Don't Eat the Marshmallow Yet (Masimelo iyagi, 2005), and Spencer Johnson and Kenneth Blanchard's Who Moved My Cheese? (Nuga nae ch'ijû rûl omgyôtsûlkka? 2000) are just a few examples.

Above all, flexibility based on individual creative customization has become a core value of the neoliberal political economy. The liberal ethos that advocates rationality, pragmatism, and cost efficiency through social harmony is manifested in the domains of daily lives not only in the planning and auditing of oneself as a profitable asset: the liberal ethos is also circulated and saturated in the care, love, and cultivation of oneself as the matrix of the self-discovery process that is necessary to identify the unique value in oneself. As a result, an individual's value in the market comes not merely through the development of a particular skill but depends on one's capacity to micromanage oneself as a whole. These processes are not perceived as coercive or as oppression from others but rather as voluntary and creative actions of empowerment, a sign of self-affirmation and self-love. Thus these self-management processes are prevalent not only in the commercialized realms but also in nonprofit organizations' self-help groups and community organizing activities (Cruikshank 1999; Joseph 2002; Li 2007).

For example, Pohûi, mentioned briefly in regard to her mother's intrusive comments, works in a women's nonprofit NGO as a coordinator of new membership programs. She noticed that interest in understanding one's own potential had increased among new members of her organization since 2000. She gave the example of the increasing popularity of psychological tests, such as Myers-Briggs Type Indicators (MBTI)[18] and Enneagram,[19] and women's leadership consulting. She said:

> They are interested in whether they need to stay in their career, if they stay, how to have a good relationship in the workplace or what would be the best kind of work for them within the company, and if not this career and workplace, what else they could do.

She added:

> It used to be that gender discrimination or the origins of women's oppression were the popular themes in our workshops. But now, women who come to our organization want to reflect on their lives through these tests and workshops [MBTI, Enneagram, and women's leadership consulting]. They go back with lots of *self-affirmations* (*chagi kûngjông*).

Pohûi herself was actively searching for self-affirmation. When she received a gift of a book for creativity development in English called *The Artist's Way* (Cameron 1992), she tried reading it (with the ambition to learn more English) but soon gave up. Then her friend bought a Korean version of the book *Aju t'ûkpyôl han chûlgôum*, which means "a very special pleasure" (Cameron 1997). She said:

> This is a book with a three months' program to teach you how to find what you want to do and want to be. It contains a pledge to yourself, ways to seek positive aspects in yourself, dates with yourself, etc. Every day you have to write a "morning page," three pages about everything every morning. Through the book, I came to see myself in a different light, and it was an opportunity to begin new things, such as card fortune-telling and photography.

Although Pohûi was positive about the self-help books, Chunhee, the woman who resisted her parents' curfew, was very critical of the self-management phenomenon. She was distressed to find that the popular self-help book *Morning-Style Person* prescribes getting up early for success. Chunhee regretted that she could not make herself into a morning person no matter how hard she tried. She advocated diverse lifestyles and a hypothetical book about "night-owl people" (*puôngi hyông in'gan*) like herself. Yet in a way, her desire to verify her own value and style was similar to the fashion of self-management.

Chunhee also suggested the Franklin Planner as a good example of self-management. The Franklin Planner is a time-management scheduler that meticulously divides weeks by days and minutes and classifies items into managed and unmanaged areas. The same author wrote a book called *The Seven Habits of Highly Effective People*. Training programs on the use of the planner and the development of personal planning skills are conducted at the Seoul branch office of the Productivity Improvement Center and Korean Leadership Center, respectively. These programs are developed for different groups of people and different versions of the planner, which targets not just businesspeople (the "executive version" and the "CEO version") but parents and students in the form of the "kid planner" and the "junior planner." This all suggests that the planning habit should be acquired at an early age. As Chunhee warned, it is very expensive: a set of planners ranges from $70 to $150, and the content must be newly purchased every year. Wondering why it is so popular despite the steep price, Chunhee affirmed that people must have a need for it; in the next minute, she doubted whether people needed it or whether it was just their fantasy or a vain hope. She was not the only interviewee who talked about the planner.

Tojin, the woman who left a women's NGO because of her low income and her qualms about the state's infiltration into the women's movement, uses the executive version of the Franklin Planner. Her women's NGO colleagues gave her the planner as a going-away gift. Although she had lived alone and supported herself since high school, she blamed herself for not being better organized. She was especially concerned about the fact that she had not made use of any "financial know-how" for saving money and securing her elderly years. As noted in chapter 2, unmarried women's anxiety in the context of postcrisis insecurity prompted many of them to become consumers of private insurance and financial products. This is a good window through which to see how the creative self-care imperative entails compulsive self-management and how the affective regime of enjoyment goes hand in hand with global financialization.

There are other examples of the way in which global financialization is combined with the social ethos of self-management and in which the combination is circulated through the affect of a flexible life and enjoyment. Chagyông, whose former male activist colleagues treated her as a deficient adult because she was unmarried, fought their insults by stating that she had at least achieved a place of her own, a self-cultivating lifestyle, and several private insurance products for future security. Her reference to her ability to adapt to the neoliberal era was a coping strategy designed to help her survive the vilification of her normative social network. And it is true that she cared for herself as a self-reliant and self-loving being; however, the moment she used the qualities of self-sufficiency and self-affirmation as grounds for being more successful than others, her actions became practices to promote neoliberal subjectivity. She also used the media's image of the successful single woman in response to her students' teasing her that they would find a husband for her. It is notable that she wanted to pass as a "hip single" (*hwaryŏ han sing'gŭl*), building on the media's representation of single women as well off and capable of managing their own lives (remember the "golden miss" and "contrasexual"), even though her situation was far from the idealized media images (Yi H-R. 2007). Chagyŏng was trying to remake her single womanhood in the image of the media's representation of single-woman status as one in which significant assets are owned. However, the majority of young unmarried women, including herself, were irregular workers with no benefits at work and no clear prospects for building assets that would secure their living, especially when they were old and unable to work.[20]

As with Chagyŏng's inadvertent reification of the neoliberal subject, Nani, the woman who quit her job due to her coworkers' constant harassment regarding her sexual identity, expressed her frustration with homeless people. Her precrisis position was that of a leftist activist's unconditional support for laborers, peasants, and other dispossessed people, expressed and undertaken in the framework of class struggle. However, since the crisis, Nani had come to question the situation of the homeless, stating that they did not make sufficient efforts to get jobs and were irresponsible about taking care of their own lives—situating herself as a citizen who was working hard to make ends meet and trying to support herself with no help from the state. By presenting herself as a more deserving citizen due to her employability and independence—an ethical justification consistent with a neoliberal subjectivity—she inadvertently gave support to the subjectivity produced by neoliberal welfare policy and public discourses.

As former leftist student activists, Chagyŏng and Nani are not naïve people who follow trends without reflection. The dilemma faced by liberalized leftist intellectuals in South Korea lies between the desire to live a flexible life not bounded by the structured capitalist employment system and the responsibility to take care of oneself in a flexible labor market. Unmarried women's pursuit of the right to be lazy and of living in their own space and time through the affective channel of affirming and caring for themselves maintains, on the one hand, a critical perspective of the "work ethic," countering Fordist capitalist production and resisting social and ideological dogmatism. On the other hand, the union of liberal ethos and affect in pursuit of a flexible life tends to endorse and buttress the neoliberal economy, particularly global financialization.

In relation to the way the liberal ethos and affect converge with neoliberal financialization, there is a notable change in the reception of the very notion of "liberal" among former student activists. Before democratization, the connotation of "liberal" was closer to "bourgeois" and had a pejorative association for leftist intellectuals. Now "liberal" has a more positive connotation among leftist intellectuals. Nani talked about the difficulty with neoliberalism:

> It was easy to identify the enemy—the capitalists and the state—in the past, when they exposed themselves so clearly. But now, my comrades [former leftist colleagues] and I say it is hard to tell who the enemies are. They are invisible, as if they have vanished, but I'm afraid that they are everywhere!

The neoliberal logic of "plasticizing" individuals to fit into unstable job markets is built into and camouflages the liberal ethos of pursuing individual freedom in the domain of the affective realm of joy, leisure, and self-affirmation. The flexible and self-sufficient labor subjectivity that South Korean leftist intellectuals viscerally developed in the process of countering the authoritarian state and Fordist capitalist production might not be effective in defying neoliberal social governing and increased insecurity in global financialization. If not, what do my research participants as rank-and-file leftist feminist workers think, and how do they maintain their integrity and balance in their activist space? With that question in mind, the last chapter returns to an affective regime inherited from the predemocratization era that is in negotiation with their current affective regime of enjoyment.

Chapter 4

Affective Baggage and Self-Suspension

⁂

Again, tonight,
the capitalist God
offers us credit
in order to earn substantial interest
from our insubstantial dream.
Ah, endless heaven no matter how far you go,
the beauty of Father's nation.

Hope flutters like tender leaves.
From somewhere the countless fruits of time
ripen and drop again.
How far must I trudge, trudge?
Why must I limp and keep going in such a dream?

I collected my sum of sadness
and cooked up a bowl of porridge with it.
Come, have some with me.

So we can take
one more energetic step
towards death.

—Ch'oe Sûng-ja, "For Suk" (translated by Don Mee Choi)

In this chapter, I focus on two kinds of affective baggage in South Korean history—the social mourning or weighty sense of social duty of the 1980s and the imperative for an enjoyable life of the 1990s. These conflicting affects circulate among and contextualize the lives of unmarried women who live on their own. The previous chapter considered the political and historical contradiction of research participants, all members of the political left who became socially liberal in their resistance to the dogmatic social norm (such as in the gender/marriage hierarchy and the overvaluing of work) through the affect of enjoyment. This affect was not just progress in the sense of emancipation but unwittingly converged with the neoliberal ethos of mediating a flexible life as a part of self-management. This chapter aims to show the potential of these women as well as the dilemma they face as lateral agents of a new ethos and a new politics because of their straddling of two very different affective regimes.[1] I demonstrate that the emotional labor they spend while working for NGOs (both paid and unpaid) combines affects from both the 1980s and the 1990s as part of an ongoing process of making a new ethics relevant to a new era—although this combination has not been selected or performed consistently by these women. The previous chapter focused on the affective domain of enjoyment used by my research participants for the self-caring technology of the self, but in this chapter, the same affective domain is viewed as a venue for self-interruption or self-suspension.

To address the complex historical background of the affective realm in South Korea, I would like to contextualize the poem that begins this chapter. It is important to come to grips with the affective domain and how affect is circulated if we are to understand how subjectivity is channeled and consolidated into a particular convergence of ideology, discourse, and ethics. Poems conveying feelings of collective mourning during the 1980s and films and TV dramas that captured the ambience of enjoying life in the 1990s were affected by the shared experiences of people in the particular historical context and, at the same time, affected the production of a particular sociopolitical subjectivity of the particular time and space.

Ch'oe Sûng-ja, a poet well-known for her poignant writing against the dictatorship and capitalism in the 1980s, dedicated this poem to a person whose name is "Suk," a common suffix for a woman's name that is used to address a person affectionately or intimately. Ch'oe's writing was rarely associated with "feminine" poetry, which in Korea is conventionally viewed as dealing with a depoliticized subject, such as nature, emotion, religion, or motherhood.[2] Her writing was seen as intellectual poetry because of her unabashedly acrid and satirical writing style.[3] Her poems were adored and acclaimed by South Korean leftist intellectuals, regardless of gender, not merely as sociopolitical criticism but as an exquisite representation of their tormented feelings in confronting the seemingly impossible task of ending the fascist military regime. Her poems—and others of the 1980s[4]—were no less significant, and perhaps more effective, than the underground Marxist study groups aimed at raising class consciousness[5] in terms of their impact on the formation of sociopolitical subjectivity.

Ch'oe's poems, loaded with the trope of death, a common one among her contemporaries, were an affective tool that enabled contemporary South Koreans' "labor of social mourning"—whether it was manifested through a lingering guilt about and sympathy for the dispossessed, tortured, or massa-cred people or through a form of participation in sociopolitical organizations directed at the goal of social change. I borrow the term of "labor of social mourning" from Loïc Wacquant (1999). Wacquant uses the term to capture the weight of structural injustice that disenfranchised people bear in their daily lives—in his case, in the impoverished ghettos in Chicago:

> Under such conditions of relentless and all-pervading social and economic insecurity, where existence becomes reduced to the craft of day-to-day survival and where one must continually do as best as one can with whatever is at hand, that is, precious little, the pres-ent becomes so uncertain that it devours the future and prohibits thinking about it except as a fantasy. And the immense labor. . . . to which Rickey [one of Wacquant's informants] must continually devote himself to make life bearable is also, in its own way, a labor of social mourning that does not say its name. (Wacquant 1999, 156).

Citing "labor of social mourning," (Berlant 2007a, 300), Laurent Ber-lant employs "living death" (2007a, 291) or "slow death (2007b, 754, 759) to refer to the daily experience of the post-Fordist era "where life building and the attrition of human life are indistinguishable" (2007b, 754). For example, in her observation of U.S. popular culture, which pathologizes obesity as abnormal and a social harm (in relation to its negative impact on work productivity), eating is both nourishment and activity motivated by stress. Building upon Harvey's (2000) critique of the capitalist under-standing of sickness as the inability to work, Berlant (2007b, 777) offers a creative analysis of a pleasure, such as eating, as both self-sustenance and self-interruption. As she explains:

> Eating is a form of ballast against wearing out; but it is also a coun-terdissipation in that, like other small pleasures, it can produce an experience of self-abeyance, of floating sideways. In this view it's not synonymous with agency in the tactical or effectual sense dedicated to self-negation or self-extension, *but self-suspension*. . . . In the model I am articulating here, the body and a life are not only projects but also sites of *episodic intermission* from personality, of inhabiting agency differently in small vacations from the will itself, which is so often

spent from the pressures of coordinating one's pacing with the pace of the working day, including times of preparation and recovery from it. (Berlant 2007b, 778–79; italics added)

The agency Berlant proposes is therefore a self-interruptive or lateral agency, which on the one hand brings pleasure, "interrupting the liberal and capitalist subject called to consciousness, intentionality, and effective will." But on the other hand, these moments of self-suspension or "small vacations of the will" often result in shifting the "sensual space between pleasure and numbness" (Berlant 2007b, 779).

Wacquant's labor of social mourning is useful in describing the deadly weight of social-emotive baggage from South Korea in the 1980s that resulted in a militant—in the sense of being aggressive and tightly organized—oppositional political movement with an experience of revolution. Further, Berlant's concept of lateral agency and self-suspension is effective in understanding the transition between affective regimes, from the sense of loss and obligation through the revolutionary period to the sense of enjoyment in the postrevolution era. The transition is not easy to pin down chronologically. Although the democratization is dated as taking place in 1987, opposition movements continued to operate until the mid-1990s. At the same time, criticism of the movements' dogmatic practices started to appear clearly in the early 1990s and intensified during the civil society movement throughout the 1990s and the new millennium.

An example of the transition to experiencing the affect of enjoyment as an act of intermission or suspension—but not as negation—is seen in an interview with poet Kim Hyesoon. Don Mee Choi, the translator of Ch'oe's poems and those of two other contemporary women poets (Kim Hyesoon [or Kim Hye-sun] and Yi Yôn-ju), discusses Kim's aesthetic in the preface to the poetry collection *Anxiety of Words*:

> Kim Hyesoon said that in the context of *minjung* [Korean subaltern] literature, her poetry did not resist directly: "What I wrote about was cooking and my ingredient was death. . . . I tried to turn the heaviness of oppression into something playful and light, so that what I ended up with was a type of poetry that did not appear to be political." (Don Mee Choi 2006, xviii)[6]

If Ch'oe's somber tone of death is representative of her contemporaries, Kim's imperative to write poems that turn heavy pathos into something "playful and light" is a precursor to the "enjoyment" that has been a salient social ethos since the mid-1990s. It is important to note that there is no clear temporal boundary between the affective regimes, as

I noted above.[7] There was playfulness in some aspects of the political and student movement culture—for example, the revitalizing of traditional folk-music bands (*p'ungmulpae*) as the repertoire of demonstrations and rallies.[8] However, this playfulness is not comparable to the liberal pleasure of more recent years, exhibited by my research participants. The "playfulness" as a thread of student movement culture was a particular kind of joy and effort in appreciating the proletarian or subaltern aesthetics that became prominent toward the late 1980s rather than a universal measurement and imperative of personal success and achievement, as in the 1990s and especially after the Asian financial crisis in the new millennium. This was a time when both the dictatorship and the student movement were worn out from rigidity and harshness, and the possibility of using enjoyment as interruption and lifestyle was more viable.

There is another example that shows the preliberalization period's pleasure-seeking phenomena, which do not fit into the periodization of transition and evince the existence of a different kind of pleasure regime, distinct from the appropriation of enjoyment as the predominant discourse (as well as affect and technologies of the self) of late capitalism (as Žižek's quote in the previous chapter reminds us). A notable infatuation with comic books, which probably began even earlier than the 1980s, has continued to the present.[9] Although there are many different genres of comic books and graphic novels, in general they are heavily influenced by Japanese manga and comic books. My informants have been exposed to gendered versions, such as melodramatic graphic novels (*sunjŏng manhwa*) since they were teenagers. Examples include *Candy Candy* (Kaendi); a translation of a Japanese teen romance, *Rose of Versailles* (Berûsaiyu ûi changmi); another Japanese epic romance based on Marie Antoinette's affair with a cross-dressing woman soldier[10]; and graphic novels drawn and written by Korean artists, such as Hwang Mi-na and Kim Hye-rin. The genre is still popular, although the subject of graphic novels has changed with the liberalization of society to include cosmopolitan lives and marginalized sexual relationships, as well as an imaginary epic genre based on premodern Korean history. Comic books sometimes share esthetics and audience with popular TV dramas. For example, *K'ôpi p'ûrinsû ilho chôm* (Coffee Prince Branch Number One) is a TV drama about an androgynous young woman in love with a man who thinks of her as a young man. It mirrors *Western Antique Cookie Shop* (Sôyang koldong yang'guaja chôm), a Japanese comic book evoking gay romantic tension that is popularly read among young women in Korea.

My research participants have followed trends within the genre for decades. For example, Hosôn, who moved out from her parents' house although she and they live in the same city, overlapped her comments on

Chosôn yôhyôngsa Tamo (Tamo: A Woman Cop in Chosôn Dynasty), an epic
TV drama aired in 2003, with her favorite comic books:

> I really really liked Tamo. I put a poster of it on my wall. I didn't
> watch *Taejangkûm* [an epic TV drama of an imaginary medicine
> woman who became the chief chef of the royal palace during
> the Chosôn dynasty; it is the most popular TV drama in Asia,
> emblematic of the "Korean wave"]. But I watched Tamo. I lived
> in the Internet because of Tamo.
>
> I liked the content and the speed. It was different from other dramas
> in that the progress was fast enough. Also, the lines of narrative
> were really refreshing. I'm not sure whether you have seen the
> drama. In the first episode there is a martial arts fight scene under
> the falling petals of an *ume* tree, and the woman cop gets hurt. In
> that scene, her boss asks her, "Are you in pain?" When she said
> "Yes," he said, "If you are in pain, I am too." It was so unexpected.
> It's more like conversations from melodramatic comic books. In
> comic books, there are lots of *caring narratives* [*paeryôha nûn taesa*].
> I like that aspect. If you asked me for one more drama, I'd say
> *Kôjinmal* [Lies]. It's about affairs or scandals. But the expressions
> in the narratives are so *beautifully set* and no one really gets hurt
> from the tormented relationships. (italics added)

Hosôn makes an aesthetic connection between comic books and TV
dramas through her affective capacity to appreciate sympathy. Comic books
developed her sentiment and affect so that she thinks of the intimate caring
style as beautiful and cathartic. This sense of *intimate caring* as enjoyable
and elating is not unrelated to what many of my research participants seek
and practice in their human relationships in friendship, family, activism, and
work. We can recall some examples. Neither Hosôn nor Minsô had much
career or life-plan ambition, but both enjoyed meeting and hanging out with
people—in Minsô's case, to the point of having trouble with her parents,
who do not understand the range and depth of her caring for nonfamily
members. Pohûi believes the self-affirming workshops held by her women's
organization laid the groundwork for successful and rewarding *care for herself*
and other women and the women's movement as a whole. Sônu was devoted
to her junior colleagues during her time as a student activist, even though
this *caring work* was criticized by her comrades as "babysitting." Thus, the
realm of caring in connection to the affect of enjoyment was present in
part in the previous area.

Although there have been these liminal or dormant zones of pleasure since the 1980s, the postdemocratization era, especially of postcrisis period, exhibited a full-fledged affective regime of enjoyment. Everyone welcomed the liberalizing political process, conflating it with democratization—including leftist student activists who used to be critical of liberalism as bourgeois ideology (see chapter 3). They too became immersed in the ethics of enjoyment as a way of denouncing the doctrinaire and patriarchal structure of their former militant, antistate activism.

Wony and Tojin were surprised by the change to an affective regime in the public sphere. Wony reflected that enjoyment was becoming much more salient in the liberalized era, especially in the environment of political activism:

> If there were individuals who stood out in student activism, they were blamed for undermining collective representation (*pandong seryôk*). It was not welcomed in the context where so-called "glorious collectivism" was a catch phrase in the student activism of my university years. For example, there was a person in my school who always came out to demonstrations but stood out because of dyed yellow hair and unique clothing, which was either too colorful or too skimpy. When people criticized the person a lot, I assumed the person was a guy, but it turned out to be a woman. But then, that kind of glorious collectivism is gone nowadays. You know what, I was very surprised when I went to the opening event of May Day [International Worker's Day] the other day [mid-2000s]. The front seats were all taken by women with high heels, pretty one-piece dresses, and fancy handbags. They were busy chatting (*suda rûl ttô nûn kô*).[11] What the heck is going on here, I wondered? It's not just one or two people. It's not even originality. It is a new trend. You know who was elected student president at Seoul National University this time? It is a totally counteractivist trend. The new student president pledged not to hold rallies in the university square. His background is diverse—he's worked as a manager of a grocery shop, a singer in a band, and an online game entrepreneur. Then, after the election, he took Seoul National University out of the activist federation of students! There are really funny things going on.

Whereas Wony lamented the changes in student activism as a sign of the influence of the new affective regime of enjoyment, Tojin, the veteran student activist and now a feminist and antiwar movement activist, bluntly asserted the need for additional changes to make the political activist scene more playful and effective. Commenting on demonstration culture in summer 2006, she said:

> I don't want to go to a rally and demonstration without being able to enjoy it, do you? It's damn hard work sitting on the pavement for hours, chanting and singing propaganda songs to the point of bruising your bum. Especially knowing that it will only merit a marginal report in the newspaper—a single line reporting that there was a traffic jam because of the rally—with no explanation of what caused the trouble.

Wony's and Tojin's 2006 narratives anticipate the unique phenomenon of the Candlelight Vigil Mass Demonstration in summer 2008 and Roh Moo Hyun's public memorial service in spring 2009, where the affective realms of social mourning and enjoyment appear together. But first it is important to address examples of lateral agency—the self-suspension that goes along with self-cultivation. The examples of lateral agency that my informants exercise are found in their narratives when they vacillate between the affective domains of social mourning and personal enjoyment. They appear unable to pin down some direction between the two or to articulate a third possibility that would provide a new activist goal and modality.

Sônu is the woman who left student activism behind after graduation and instead joined a leftist women's NGO. She participates in a variety of group activities in the organization and does English-Korean translation for the organization. When I asked if her NGO activities were related to her leftist desire for social change, she answered,

> Well, yes, it is related. I think it's for self-respect [as a leftist member]. I can say I still have a passion [for social change] that helps me to carry on. When I tried to earn money through translation for a big company, I felt less rewarded than I do with my translation work for the women's organization, although it was an identical application of my English skill. Some companies have the image of advocating for the common good. But I still feel it's not as rewarding as helping NGOs. I felt compromised working for a capitalist, profit-oriented company; it made me feel disgusted with the world and myself. That didn't give me any pleasure.

Sônu, finding her relatively stable company job capitalistic and boring, sought enjoyment through travel and eventually discovered a passion for translation. Her joining and helping the NGO is the embodiment of an activist mind inherited from the activist history of the 1980s, but her appreciation of individual freedom and joy also resulted from her critique of the collective political activism she was involved with when she attended university. When she compared herself to her former colleagues, she was critical about their lives:

> It is hard to be involved with political activism while preparing to enter a secure job market. Even with preparation, it's not easy to obtain a job. You end up being a parasite on your parents. So former student activists cannot adjust properly to social life [*sahoe chôkûng*]. I don't object to the life of political activists. It would be nice if we could live such a life, because it is such a courageous one with many challenges. But I find them living a life of grieving their loss or nostalgia for past activism rather than being realistic and living a new life. Many former student activists don't try new things.

Exploring a new career as a translator enabled Sônu to join a new affective community whose members knew how to enjoy life or at least made the effort to do so. It is important to note that the way in which she used enjoyment, such as quitting her job to travel, brought an abrupt interruption to her life subsistence and security. If we see her action to give in to the joy of traveling as impulsive, not practical or realistic, how is it different from the colleagues she criticizes for suspending their lives in the past affect of mourning? The difference would be that she suspended her life in the pleasure of the moment rather than being stuck in nostalgia for the past. Neither is 100 percent practical or realistic. Sônu's case was more hopeful in terms of seeking new experience, but there was no guarantee that the risk-taking would be practical in terms of gaining subsistence.[12]

When we recall Berlant's conceptualization of lateral agency, we can see that suspension of life through pleasure is not disavowal but essential to and simultaneous with life building. This is especially true for people who are paralyzed between limited job options and the growing flexibility of the ever-more-capitalist world that gauges everything by its value-producing ability. This frame helps us to understand Sônu's ambivalent attitude to the meaning of her membership in the women's NGO:

> Am I still involved in activism? I cannot easily answer that. I don't know if it's necessary to be an activist all the time. I don't think I am an activist. If you ask me, "What is activism?" in my opinion, it requires, at minimum, being a staff person or a "brain" [strategist] in an activist organization. I feel that it is not enough to call myself an activist if I am just a volunteer in an organization. Once

I was thinking about being a staff member. But I couldn't think of myself doing it, because it is so labor intensive in relation to the wage. Further, there is no time for self-development.

The fact that Sônu does not want to be a staff person indicates that her self-cultivation and personal enjoyment take priority over the collective imperative. At the same time, she has a high expectation of what it means to be an activist or someone who deserves the title, out of respect to the other affective regime of social duty, and she feels guilty for not being able to carry it out fully. Sônu's ambivalence suspends her decision making and her identity at the risk of not attaining anything concrete in the near future in terms of life building. This type of lateral agency in relation to their labor for women's organizations and movements is common among my research participants.

We can remember Tojin's frustration about being unable to make ends meet after a decade of working in an established women's NGO. Although her ideal of making a living as a political activist was dampened when she quit, she also felt liberated when she followed her impulse and showed her dissatisfaction with the poor wages and working conditions. Pohûi, the membership coordinator in a women's organization, worked at a variety of part-time jobs—such as fortune-telling in a café, facilitating MBTI and Enneagram workshops, and selling insurance products—to supplement her full-time salary of less than $1,000 a month.

It is not surprising that conditions for temporary NGO workers are even worse than those for regular NGO workers. Wony noted that temporary staff in women's NGOs were hired through public works programs and paid minimum wage following the Asian financial crisis. The government sponsored NGO programs in the name of creating social enterprises (*sahoe chôk kiôp*) or social employment (*sahoe chôk iljjari*). Wony was concerned about the labor conditions of the highly educated women who were working for these NGO-customized public works programs at wages on average of 600,000 to 700,000 won (approximately $600–$700) per month. These kinds of public works programs in women's NGOs were the ones that Pohûi, Togyông, and Tojin were hired for when they first moved from the countryside to Seoul.[13]

Wony points out that working for NGOs is not merely a matter of making the minimum wage; it is also gendered care work (assigned to women)—such as day care and hospice work—that is low paying despite the high-quality skills needed. My research participants' jobs in general, whether they were paid or volunteer, relied heavily on the caring quality of the labor, attending to emotional needs and requiring sensibility and emotional effort.[14] Pohûi's perception of what new members want and how self-love is the foundation of self-affirmation from her experience of facilitating personality tests is a good example. In addition to the fact that these jobs require a caring quality, my research participants' affective regime is deeply influenced by the aesthetics of care manifested in melodramatic comic books and recent TV dramas. Thus, my research participants appreciate, practice, and circulate their affective baggage of social duty through care and immaterial work as the core of their gendered labor and activism.

There are a number of paradoxes in these single women's care labor. Although they are caring for the needs of members of the women's organization, they do not think that it is possible to put their own issues—like the housing difficulties they experience as unmarried women—on the political agenda of their women's NGOs. Rather, they feel obliged to work in women's groups oriented toward normative and mainstream women's issues, such as marriage and reproduction and public day care for married working women with children. To be fair, day-care issues are very relevant, particularly in the last few years, as South Korea's "low fertility and aging society" (*chôchulsan koryônghwa*) has become a public and official concern.[15] As Tojin says,

> Roh Moo Hyun's [former president, 2003–2008] pledge during the election was, "Give birth to a child, then I'll be responsible for its child care and education." But look, he is deregulating child-care fees now. In the era of "low fertility and aging society," without state support such as a public child-care system, who would want to give birth unless they are insane? Especially now, as 70 percent of women are working as unstable [irregular, part-time] workers.

However, when the research participants were asked whether they thought their own situation was an issue that could be taken up by the women's movement, Tojin and others were surprised. They admitted that they had not thought about it much but said that they did not feel that other activists or married feminist activists would see unmarried women's housing as an urgent issue that would garner wide solidarity. Hosôn's narrative, quoted in the Introduction, explains this marginalization of single women because of the government emphasis on low fertility. As she says, "If anyone raises an issue of single women's needs in this context, they wouldn't take it seriously, no way (ssi to an môkil kôt kat ta)."

Pohûi, the advocate of self-affirmation, concurs, saying, "We would have been deemed spoiled rats if we demanded things for unmarried women from the state." Kyuri ranked the issues within the women's movement in this way: "[Middle-aged, married] women heads of family (yôsông kajang) would be the top priority, and single women uninterested in marriage would be the bottom." It is ironic that only nonsingle women merit the classification of head of household, even though many single women, such as Kyuri, are heading households in poverty or, like Chagyông and Sônu, taking care of their ailing parents until they die. Moreover, the labor for social repro-duction and social change that most of my research participants put in as single women is not accounted for.

My research participants are not uncritical and accepting of the con-vention of marginalizing single women's issues in the women's movement. As Wony says,

> I'm uneasy with the way in which women's organizations and movements consider married women's motherhood and day care as representative of women's issues, appealing to people's imagination by describing the pain of mothers and married working women. I know they are in a challenging situation. But they are not the only ones who are in need. They chose to be married and have children. I'm tired of people's assumption that I will do research on child care for married women workers if I say I'm interested in women's labor issues. Because government money is released to solve the problem of low fertility, women's organizations get more funding for that. But I don't know what women's organizations can do to increase birth rates. Maybe marry more and give birth to more babies? I was quite puzzled to find a famous liberal women's cultural organization facilitating a two-year program called "Goodbye Solo" as part of the Gender Equality Ministry's campaign for a "caring society" (tolbom sahoe). I was perplexed to see the title, thinking the women's organization went too far in providing a dating program. But it is actually about building a women's community. Still, I think the title entails confusion and misunderstanding.

Consciousness about single women's issues is slowly growing. A young feminist webzine pushed for the single women's movement to host the Pihon Yôsông Festival in 2007, and many new books have been written about unmarried women's needs and challenges. In addition, there have been some attempts to address single women's issues after my interviews, although I do not know if it is coincidental or possibly because of the interviews. Most forums and symposiums held over the last few years have focused on single-woman parenthood rather than on housing. Yet single women's needs have not been recognized to the point of making them an item on the women's movement policy agenda. So far, there are no campaigns to remove age and marriage regulations from housing loan policies or countermovements to the low fertility propaganda that would redirect the focus of care from women's reproduction to nurturing the neglected population.[16]

If the low fertility issue is an example of my research participants' collective needs being silenced without much resistance on their part (an example of their self-suspension while seeking more favorable moments), the new demonstration culture exhibited in 2008 and 2009 indicates that there is potential for these politically leftist and socially liberal women to balance their affective baggage. Tojin's and Wony's comments in 2006 on the new trends in political activism anticipated some unusual political events, such as the Candlelight Vigil Mass Demonstration in Seoul during the summer of 2008.[17]

The demonstration, recording the largest participation since the 1987 democratization rally, was held to protest the South Korean government's tepid response to complaints about the questionable quality of imported U.S. beef (suspected of being tainted by "mad cow" disease). The demonstration is unique in the history of antistate activism in Korea in two aspects. First, it was unprecedented in terms of its festive and convivial ambience, at least during the first two months.[18] Although there were mass candlelight vigils before 2008 as a form of political protest, such as the 2002 candlelight vigil against U.S. military presence in South Korea after a U.S. Army vehicle accident that killed two young women, the affective environment of those candlelight vigils had a far from bright or celebratory ambience (Jiyeon Kang

"Young Demonstrators at Candlelight Vigil in 2008." Source: *Han'gyôre*, May 23, 2008. Photo by Seung hwa Park.

2012). In the vigil of 2008, there were families with baby strollers and carri-ers, women in their twenties with high heels and fashionable clothing who had met each other through Internet blogs on cosmetic surgery or fashion (similar scenes of which had shocked Wony a few years earlier), and groups of women in their thirties and forties, including housewives affiliated with healthy food campaigns, aerobic dance, and football teams.[19] The music and dances performed at the demonstration were not the serious propaganda-styled songs sung at movement gatherings in the past (*undongkwon kayo* or *minjung kayo*) or traditional folk music (*p'ungmulpae*). Rather, they were mild political songs, such as *"achim isŭl"* (Morning Dew),[20] and recreational music and dances for children. People compared the festive spectacle of the Candlelight Vigil to the mass cheering at the 2002 FIFA World Cup game between Korea and Japan (when a mass of Koreans wore red in support of their team). This kind of enjoyable demonstration might be common else-where in the world, but Korean mass demonstrations are generally militant and charged even when they are peaceful. Before the 2008 Candlelight Vigil, the seriousness of political concerns and the heavy tension caused by facing suppression by the state police force was the dominant public feeling.

Another characteristic of the Candlelight Vigil is that it did not have any central leadership and surprised everyone with its wide spectrum of participants in regard to gender, age, region, social affiliation (groupings through the Internet, neighbor sports, and other connections), and class. Critics noted that established civil society movement organizations (such as *Chinboyŏndae* [People's Solidarity for Social Progress], *Minjunochong* [Korean Confederation of Trade Unions], and *Chamyŏyŏndae* [People's Solidarity for Participatory Democratization]) did not win people's support (Seo 2008a, 2008b; Yŏ 2008). It is common to see the situation as a failure of civil society movement organizations, and it engendered a great deal of self-criticism among intellectuals.[21] The fact that a variety of people, including housewives and young women, demonstrated around issues of the politics of living and food was highlighted in contrast to the conventional confronta-tional demonstration by masculinized elite college students and intellectuals that marked the preliberalization era.[22] I would like to think of the lack of effective leadership as not necessarily a failure but a sign of the suspension of a dormant political group—a movement in the liminal stage of seeking new directions in political affects and ethos.

Some might describe it as a "quiet" revolution.[23] Although the most striking population that joined the demonstration was young people in their teens or twenties—also central figures in the World Cup event (Joo 2012)—it is crucial to pay attention to the dormant power of rank-and-file intellectuals like my research participants, who experienced both affective regimes close up. The fact that they lived through the transition period to democratization makes their experience unique; it impelled them to come up with a hybrid version of political leftist and social liberal personal politics. This would not have been so easy for the previous generation or the later generation, both of whom were exposed mainly to one affective regime during their youth and young adult period.

It is true that there has been criticism of the generation that lived through the transition, dubbed *sam p'al yuk sedae* since the 1990s. The term, literally meaning "generation of 386," describes former student activists who led leftist movements for the Korean subaltern: in their thirties (3), attended universities in the 1980s (8), and born in the 1960s (6) (N. Lee 2007, 301).[24] Many former student movement leaders became mainstream politicians, and rank-and-file former student activists disappeared into adult lives that became compromised with and complacent about the liberal and consumerist capitalist world of the 1990s.[25] However, this criticism of the rank-and-file activists of the previous era needs to be contested, because their alleged disappearance, along with the downfall of radical political movements, can be understood as *self-suspension*, not as disavowal or betrayal. Ample examples in the narratives of unmarried women who are rank-and-file members of this generation show that their self-suspension derived from a mixture of disappointment with their former activist experience; some soul searching about their own vision and value; and deliberation about a new appreciation of personal space, including the freedom for single women to live alone. These women are simmering in the new space of the politically left and socially liberal, quietly overriding the predominant forces of either the politically right and socially liberal (such as the conservative state regimes, in conjunction with the neoliberal market) or the politically left and socially conservative (such as masculinist former student activists).

Self-suspension is essential to the life building of self and society, especially in the aftermath of the revolutionary era. Revolution as a critical event does not bring solutions and changes in reality automatically and spontaneously, even though it is the result of long-term collective efforts and contingencies. Rather, it tends to bring political depression and a vacuum of radical ideas and activities because of the presence of a counter-revolutionary force (Elyachar and Winegar 2012). In this context, we need to understand that the dormant potential of these rank-and-file revolutionary members is the very fact that they are taking time to brew new politics through intermission and self-suspension. These people do not want or need to have intellectuals or activist leaders tell them what to do. They are seeking articulation of their own so they can explain their mixed heritage of affect and ethos in their political and individual lives. They are trying to differentiate neoliberal capitalist tactics from the liberal democratic agenda, as Nani reveals in her confusion about identifying "enemies" (see chapter 3). My research participants are expressing their dissatisfaction that activist organizations are not operating independently from the state or are not updating their strategies to new affective needs as they risk losing institutional ground for their activist identities. Tojin and Wony left their respective women's organizations, and Sônu is reluctant to make a strong commitment to the women's NGO. In their daily lives, they are defying the denigration of single women's adulthood and the curbs on their residential liberty via personal, familial, and social networks—in spite of their judgment that the current focus on low fertility means it is not the best time to present their political demands to the state. They are actively shaping the boundaries of their individual space at the same time that they are mending their relationships with their natal families and social networks or seeking a new community that they can rely on, as Chisu and Minsô show. They are also struggling to find ways in which they can financially secure their elderly years as single women with rare benefits and below-average income from precarious employment—although most of them do not seem to be putting together the picture of how sedimented and global financializations constrain them as a financially vulnerable population.

In terms of sedimented financialization, my research participants grumble but have not yet tried collectively to challenge the way in which the entrenched lump-sum cash transaction system of rental housing in South Korea is combined with discriminatory state and bank loan policies. Thus they have few options but to rely on their families and risk being under their sexual and moral control. Global financialization is still embryonic, yet it is salient in the daily lives of my research participants, as demonstrated by their adherence to the rhetoric of asset-building techniques and financial know-how (chaetekû) (despite the fact that it is a modest scope of finance compared to middle-class participation in the stock and mortgage markets). Is this a sign of lack of resistance, as some South Korean intellectuals claim?

Kang Chun-man (2000), a potent social critic of former military dictators and conservative newspaper columnists, has criticized South Koreans for giving up their opposition to sociopolitical injustice, saying, "Why did people lose their indignation? The thought that they have stopped resisting enrages me." However, I do not believe the people have lost their indignation just because they have been seeking some enjoyment in their lives or because their power or their type of defiance does not surface militantly on a mass scale. Rather, people like my research participants are suspending and recharging themselves, refusing to give in to simplistic optimism or to use explicit expressions. Chunhee aptly describes this:

Democratization did not solve the problems of capitalism in South Korea. Rather, it seems to have provoked capitalism further. Actually, I do not hear the word "democratization" that often anymore. I suspect that liberal democratization and acceleration of capitalism are almost interchangeable terms.

It is in this place of suspicion and suspension that my research participants, as lateral agents, assert the potential for the development of a new affect and ethos in post-revolutionary South Korean politics.

Notes

Introduction

1. "Ssi to an môkil kôt kat ta" literally means "even a seed would not be accepted [not to mention a full plant or tree]."

2. Youth unemployment issues were presented in South Korea as an individual problem. South Korean youth were pressed to survive the employment crisis through their own self-sufficiency and creativity, and the government showcased entrepreneurs who successfully commodified their ideas in the information technologies (IT) markets (Song 2009b). For example, a special report on four individuals who found employment abroad through self-promotion on the Internet highlights three qualifications: ideas (or dreams), expertise, and English (Kim Ki-hwan 2011).

3. A global student strike in November 2012 was not as successful as the Occupy movement. Also, it is notable that despite the support for local and global protests after 2008, there have been cautious and critical observations about the romanticizing of revolutionary events, particularly in the context of the Arab Spring, that do not seem to be accompanied by thoughts on the post-revolutionary process or even counterrevolutionary movements. See Elyachar and Winegar's (2012) note on Egypt before the summer of 2013, which proved their concerns were accurate.

4. For information about the situation in Québec, see Peritz (2012), Yakabuski (2012). For Greece and Europe, see Sotiris (2012), Wagenknecht (2012). For the Arab Spring, see McNally (2011b).

5. The gendered labor experience in South Korea is similar to that in other countries. See Kyounghee Kim (2009) for the context in South Korea, Vosko (2000) and Winson and Leach (2002) for Canada, Barry (2007) for the United States, and Hochschild (1983) and Lawson (2007) for the general context.

6. See chapter 1 for research participants' concerns about their sexual safety and their opinions on the limited public awareness about women's sexuality.

7. Karen Ho (2010) and Zaloom (2004) show they are also vulnerable to stress, risk, and unpredictability.

8. See Hulchanski (2007) and Hulchanski and Shapcott (2004) for challenges regarding rental housing in a global (especially Canadian) context from the perspective of tenants and urban rights. However, these sources do not address the possibility of rental housing as the crux of the financial market for housing.

9. "Low-income people" refers to households ranging loosely from the working-poor class to the lower middle class.

10. They were active during their university years, which ranged from the early to the mid-1990s. South Koreans tend to consider people who went to university or college in the 1980s as the core of the student activist generation (see chapter 4 for *sam pal yuk* generation), because the democratization that ended the military regimes officially took place in 1987. However, the following two governments (1987–1997) were led by a former military general and a civilian president supported by military forces. Therefore, the anti–military state movement continued until the mid-1990s.

11. According to Foucault (1988), technologies of the self "permit individuals to effect by their own means or with the help of others a certain number of operations on their own bodies and souls, thoughts, conduct, and way of being, so as to transform themselves in order to attain a certain state of happiness, purity, wisdom, perfection, or immortality" (p. 18).

12. Mental illness and suicide among former activists and civilians who were victims of state violence are receiving more attention. I learned this through experts' opinions, which include my personal conversation (February 7, 2010) with Professor Kim Dong-Choon, who served on the Truth and Reconciliation Commission until 2009, and my interview (October 8, 2009) with Dr. Jung Hye-Shin, psychiatrist and psychotherapist, who is well-known for specializing in sessions with victims of state violence.

13. See Chun-man Kang (2000) to get a sense of observations and assumptions about inertia and lack of passion for social change in the new generation. See Kyunghyang Sinmun Special Report Team (2008) for wider concerns on democracy derailed or not yet arrived and on suspended revolution among former student activisits.

14. See chapter 4 for a full elaboration of self-suspension, with Berlant's concept of "lateral agency."

15. The source of the 2005 statistics is customized data that the author purchased from the Korea Statistics Promotion Institute on June 1, 2010. Although the raw data was collected from the national census, the census did not combine the variables of marriage status; residential type by yearly lease/monthly rent/ownership; gender; and age of individuals who live by themselves.

16. See Standing (2011) for a resonant discussion of precarious workers and the new poor as an emerging class on a global scale.

17. Jessop (1994) explains that post-Fordism is a capitalist mode that tends both to destabilize labor markets and the means of production and to stabilize institutions, rules, and norms. If Fordism is exemplified by the assembly line system, a

solidly regulated mode of mass production, post-Fordism is illustrated by an unstable service and information industry. Hart and Negri (2004) equate immaterial labor to affective labor in their understanding of neoliberal empire and the potential of multitudes to counter it.

18. See Barraclough (2009) and Janice Kim (2009) for studies of pre–Korean War women factory workers.

19. In the 2000 census, university graduation was 38.9 percent for women and 62.1 percent for men. In the 2005 census, the gender ratio changed to 41.5 percent for women and 58.5 percent for men.

20. See S-K.Cho (1999) and Kim C-S. et al. (2007). Kim C-S. et al. reveals the differing employment rates between men and women with university degrees. For young adults (20 to 34 years old), 83.3 percent of men but only 66.6 percent of women were employed. For adults (over 35 years old), the figures were 91.7 percent of men and 55 percent of women.

21. Even in the changed social environment in South Korea, women's average age for first marriage was still twenty-four in the 2005 census. However, for university-educated women, the age for first marriage was almost twenty-nine years. This corresponds to the narratives of my research participants, who talked about the intense marriage pressure they felt before they were or around the time they reached that age of thirty. See chapter 1.

22. See Nicola Anne Jones (2006) for details of the harassment by Confucian conservative organizations of members of progressive women's organizations who advocated the abolition of the family headship system from 1999 to 2005 (pp. 82–83, 141–44).

23. See Republic of Korea (2010) for the second platform for 2011 to 2015.

24. See Choo (2013), Caren Freeman (2011), M. Kim (2009), Tsujimoto (forthcoming), and Paik (2011) for a discussion of migrant brides married to Korean peasants. The migrant brides were required to enroll in Korean language and cooking classes (to learn how to make kimchi). However, structural protections for the brides are insubstantial. The marriages, arranged via commercial agents, have produced a devastating economic and social power imbalance, and in some cases, the women have been murdered by their Korean husbands.

25. See Gage (2007) and Keller (2003) for the biracial Korean issue; Eleana Kim (2010, 2012) and Dorow (2006) for the adoptees' case; Hyun Ok Park (2011), Kyung Tae Park (2008), June Hee Kwan (2013), and Caren Freeman (2011) for the case of Korean Chinese; and Soo-Jung Lee (2011) and Eunyoung Choi (2010) for North Korean refugees.

26. See Joo (2012), Jun (2012), and Vogel (2011) for the situation of non-Korean migrant workers in the context of the policy and public discourse of multiculturalism.

27. These state-sponsored efforts to boost reproductive rates prepared the ground for the scandal of Hwang U-sŏk's fabricated stem-cell research data, exposed in 2006. Hwang was a world-renowned biotechnologist and medical doctor who offered hope for treating sterility. His research was supported by the presidential office and the science ministry. Even after the government and his own university

trashed his reputation and cut off their financial support for his research, women, mainly housewives, continued to attend rallies in his support.

28. From now on, "house ownership" refers to ownership of a condominium and "rental housing" refers to a rented apartment in a condominium unit or in a multiple-residence house.

29. "Briefing Asian Economies" (2009), 76.

30. Regarding the informal economy, see Keith Hart (2009), Elyachar (2010), and Quijano (2000) for non-western urban contexts; Roitman (2007) and Chaterjee (2011, especially 208–34) for nonwestern rural contexts; and Portes, Castelles, and Benton (1989), Sassen (2000), and Tabak (2000) for mostly advanced market economies. Also, see Stack (1974), among others, about the way in which kinship has been a significant resource for rearing children and circulating in-kind goods under economic/financial pressures in African American families. For information on women's participation in the informal sector that contributes to the household and national economy, see Barrow (1988), Bolles (1996), Carla Freeman (2000, 2007), and Kathryn Ward (1990), mostly about Caribbean contexts. For the informal sector utilized by the poor, see Roy (2011), Davis (2004), Keith Hart (2009), and Quijano (2000).

31. The notion of the subaltern derives from Antonio Gramsci but has been expanded by postcolonial (particularly South Asian) scholars. It is a new conceptualization of the proletariat that includes peasants and people occupying socially vulnerable positions in colonized social contexts.

32. It is debatable whether money, as the means of circulation of capital itself, has the inherent capacity to produce capital in the process of accelerating the circuit of capital accumulation. Harvey (1976 [2007]) notes this possibility as a feature of capitalism, but Graeber (2011) provides a different view. Although, like Harvey, he agrees with other Marxists that the current financial markets' far from real value-based economy is the ground of the current capitalist crisis, Graeber shows, based on ethnographic data, that debt and credit practices existed long before capitalism. Graeber thereby counters the teleological view of economic history that sees the barter system existing prior to capitalism and the creation of money in the capitalist system as a necessary device to resolve the inconvenience of economic exchange from the barter system.

33. Eun Mee Kim (1997), Woo-Cumings (1999).

34. The concept of "the labor of social mourning" was developed by Loïc Wacquant (1999) and taken up by Laurent Berlant (2007a).

Chapter 1

1. The male intellectuals included Kim Chi-ha (an influential leftist intellectual and poet), Kim Yong-ok (a philosopher of Eastern religion), and Ma Kwang-su (a literature professor who wrote sensational novels portraying women simply as sexual objects).

2. Yi Yu-Jin (2007).

3. Neo-Confucian ideology has been present in South Korea since the late Chosôn period of the seventeenth century. For the gendered history of the

Chosŏn dynasty, see Haboush (1991) and Deuchler (1992). Jung's (2009) work is an exception. For more detail on the current practices of Confucian family, gender, and marriage conventions, see Janelli and Janelli (1982) and Kendall (1996).

4. According to a 2008 survey from the National Statistics Office, 33.3 percent of women in Seoul consider marriage to be optional, compared to only 22.8 percent of men in the city (National Statistics Office 2009).

5. An estimated quarter of South Koreans are Christian. South Korea sponsors missionaries in Africa, Central Asia, and Muslim countries. See Han (2010), Baker (2008).

6. J-K. Park (2008), H. Choi (2009), and Hwang (2009).

7. See Chung (1990) for the gender conservativism in this mixture of religions from the perspective of women's emancipation theology.

8. Korean feminist scholars note that gender equality or labor rights in law and policy in South Korea were implemented by the state before women's movements arose, which explains why those laws and policies were conservative and why even existing laws and policies were not exercised in real life, for example, maternity leave. See Cho (1996) and Yang H. (2004).

9. See Ronald and Nakano (2013) for Japanese contemporary single women's situation.

10. See Hyaeweol Choi (2009), Kyeong-Hee Choi (1999), Kim Su-jin (2008), Sang-Kyung Lee (1997, 2009), and Jiwon Shin (2002) for the gender politics of Korean new women in the 1920s and 1930s. See Sato (2003) for similar phenomena in Japan and Barlow (2004) for China.

11. See Hughes (2011, 2012), and McHugh and Abelmann (2005) for information about the short-lived liberal era of the 1950s–1960s.

12. See Karen Kelsky's (2001) book on Japanese young people's cosmopolitan trends, including traveling.

13. Current domestic TV programs and movies also reflect cosmopolitan, liberal ideas. I address this topic in chapter 3.

14. The sexual politics that emerged in the early 1990s influenced the film festivals, along with the influence of underground groups devoted to the films of Jim Jarmusch, Neil Jordan, Roman Polanski, and Sergei Eisenstein. Although these began with rather grassroots scales, the mainstreaming of the film festivals was similar to the pattern of cultural festivals—such as the Independent Art Festival—that began on campuses (Shinchon is famous).

15. Busan's hosting of film festivals is part of the city's "branding" project, seen by many scholars as a key aspect of neoliberalization of city governance—the disconnecting of municipal governance from central government financial support. See Kevin Ward (2006) for business improvement projects as a part of branding cities in the western context and Hae (1999) for examples of Korean municipal branding efforts via city festivals.

16. See Jones (2006) for the mainstreaming of the women's movement in the democratized era, especially the Kim Dae Jung era (p. 202).

17. On March 10, 2007, the Pihon Festival, a feminist event, was hosted by Ŏn'nine dot.com, a young generation feminist portal site at www.unninet.net

that has led the popularization of the term *pihon yŏsŏng* in the context of promoting the independence of young women (Sŏng C-h. 2008). The Ŏn'nine webzine advertisement site is at http://www.unninet.net/plaza/plaza_newsdata_vw.asp?sidx=59 (accessed May 25, 2013). Ŏn'nine participants have also produced multiple books, such as the *Ŏn'nine pang* (Sister's Room) series (Ŏn'nine 2006, 2007, 2009, Kim Hyŏn-jin 2009). A similar feminist book on "independence" in South Korea is *Na, tongnip han ta* (I am going to live independently, Kim Hŭi-su et al. 2007), which does not focus only on unmarried women, published by Ilda Press, a sister organization that has another young feminist webzine, ildaro.com.

18. See Sang-Kyung Lee (1997, 2009) and Kyeong-Hee Choi (2001) for the predicament of women resisting marriage and family in the 1920s as reflected in leftist and liberal literature.

19. Kwon Myŏng-ah's *Muhanhi chŏngch'i chŏk in ôiroum* (Boundless Political Solitude) (2012) examines the contemporary political isolation and affects of single women by analyzing popular culture and single women's best sellers over the last two decades.

20. My own experience of being a freelance translator during the crisis supports this story. See Song (2009b).

21. Sojŏng's perception of the job market reflects the increasing unemployment rate since the crisis. However, according to S-K Cho (1999), it is a myth that women's employment rate was much higher before the crisis. Cho's claim is supported in that Sojŏng's older sister's peer group, including Sŏnu (see chapters 3 and 4), or even her own cohorts with less prestigious university degrees, such as Chunhee, had difficulties getting jobs even prior to the crisis. At the same time, both Sŏnu and Chunhee noted that low-wage jobs in small companies were available throughout the crisis. Both of them left jobs during the crisis, not because of low wages but because of uncomfortable human relations, including poor gender dynamics, and the boredom of repetitive office work.

22. I use the label of lesbian (*lejŭbiŏn* in Korean) following my research participants' own identification with same-sex–loving women. They also use the term *iban yŏsŏng*: the meaning is closer to "queer women" because it includes both women who prefer a same-sex relationship and bisexual women.

23. In the Korean patriarchal/patrilineal tradition, the oldest child is most responsible for dealing with inheritance and caring for the parents. Although the inheritance traditionally goes to the eldest son, even if a daughter is older, the common expectation is that the first child of any gender is responsible for caring for parents and younger siblings.

24. There is a new phenomenon of urbanites, including young single women, deciding to get involved in (usually environmentally friendly) farming. Although it is beyond the scope of this book, which focuses on young single women's residential options in the urban context, farming life is becoming a more important option for some young single women on whom the pressure to marry is similar to that on the women in this book. See *Diary of Returning to Farming* (Kwŏn and Im 2011). Also, see *Song of Acclamation for Farmers* (2009–2013) for young adults' settlement in countryside farming life. It is notable that the dominant image on this program of the returning population is that of young men.

25. This comment on family as something to be avoided was also noted by Chagyông, who quoted "Family is my shit" from *The Family Cinema*, written by Yu Mi-ri, a Korean-Japanese writer. According to Yu, it is an apt expression, because our shit is dirty, but it still belongs to or comes from us. The difference between Chagyông and Minsô is that Chagyông detests her family; Minsô claims that she does not dislike her family.

26. Kim Y-S. (2007).

27. Thanks to volunteer counselors from the Korean Lesbian Counseling Center (*Han'guk lejûbiôn sangdamso*) for providing this information.

28. A residential village of bar hostesses is a bit different from a red-light district (*hongdûng ka*) in that the former refers to the women's residence rather than their business area, although they sometimes overlap. For information about red-light districts and the lives of sex workers in Korea, see Cheng (2002, 2005), Park Hyejung (2008), and Yea (2005).

29. The monthly neighborhood meeting is organized by the municipal residential administration or ward office (*tongsamuso*), a Cold War product that began as a neighborhood surveillance system under the anticommunist military regime. It corresponded to North Korea's rank-and-file five-person groups (*ohodamdangje*).

30. Chôn (2006).

Chapter 2

1. Amounts in U.S. dollars are approximated throughout the book for the convenience of readers. Unless there is a separate note, "dollars" always means U.S. dollars.

2. See the website of the Korean Statistical Information Service (http:// kosis.kr/) under "Chôn'guk ch'ongjosa in'gu ch'ong'gual: si-do, sông, yôllyông pyôl" (national census data, with categories of city, province, gender, and age). Accessed August 14, 2013.

3. See Chang (2006) and Harvey (2005) for the hegemony of financial capital in the neoliberal global era. See Harvey (2005) and Lapavitsas (2009) for the definition of financialization.

4. Engels (1979) warned in the late nineteenth century that a strategy advocated by a socialist group known as the Proudhonists—that the working class should focus on gaining (equal) rights of home ownership and on getting bank loans for workers for home ownership—was flawed. Engels argued that this would end up placing workers under an eternal burden of debt, especially for those left with poor-quality housing units. Engels insisted that the only way to resolve housing problems for the working class was to get rid of classes, allowing workers to appropriate the full value of their production without being exploited by capitalists. Although the Proudhonists' proposal sounds much more practical, Engels's analysis is surprisingly accurate in the context of the 2008–2009 U.S. subprime mortgage crisis. His dire prediction has been borne out: the seemingly beneficial inclusion of the working class in house ownership on the basis of housing loans lent out by credit patrons (U.S. banks, in the case of the subprime crisis) has wound up devastating workers' housing security.

5. See Crotty and Lee (2005a, 2005b) for their definition of "financialization"

in the Korean context.

6. Eun Mee Kim (1997), Woo-Cumings (1999).

7. Haein said she wants to move from her office-tel to a regular rental apartment, but she does not have enough lump-sum cash to achieve her dream. Her complaints against the constraints of the loan market are addressed later in this chapter.

8. The Ministry of Land, Transport, and Maritime Affairs' (MLTM's) national housing fund (see "Land Housing: National Housing Fund Raising" at https://stat. molit.go.kr/portal/cate/engStatListPopup.do, accessed August 6, 2013) records that single households are excluded in principle from groups that qualify for rental housing loans. In addition, *2008 nyôndo chutaek chonghap kyehwoek an* (the National Housing Plan in 2008), the guide for lending (applied since February 25, 2008) provided by Nonghyôp chunganghoe bank, notes that borrowers must be more than thirty-five years old in the case of a single person living alone, but only more than twenty years old for nonsingle households (such as married couples). The priority for newlywed couples (and the aging segment of the population) is continued in the Housing Plan proposed by the MLTM in 2008 (for example, low-income couples married for less than five years, with a housing savings account and children, have priority). The need to accommodate diverse households was noted in a single sentence but connected to no concrete plan.

9. Although it may be seen as a kind of mortgage, the precrisis housing loan, called *chutaek tambo taechul*, operates very differently from the way the mortgage system works in North America. A North American mortgage can be lent before, or as a condition of, the purchase of real estate with up to 95 percent of the housing price. Prior to the crisis, in Korea, banks lent up to 70 percent of the purchase price of the property only after the property sale had closed. It was rare to get a loan for 70 percent, however, which reinforced the need for a significant amount of lump-sum cash elsewhere (30 percent to 50 percent of the real estate price) to be able to apply for a housing loan.

10. Although the housing loan situation has changed since the crisis by incorporating a mortgage system, the housing savings account system functions the same way it always did. There is no guarantee of owning a house through the account, but participants do have priority in entering the purchase market by using a random chance method, called *sunwûi*, which requires years of waiting and is based on whether or not one already owns a condominium. Some see the South Korean state as a paternalistic nation which has made public housing available with a housing savings account and by providing relatively cheap housing through a state-affiliated housing construction company (*chutaek kongsa*). However, unlike other nations, such as Singapore and Hong Kong, whose governments actually guarantee public housing at state expense, the South Korean government has never provided large amounts of public housing or prioritized household loans for housing.

11. This is related to Korean gift culture, which I discuss further on.

12. I asked five major credit card companies and four secondary financial institutions (run by either banks or big corporations) to explain their policies in April and May 2010. They tended to deny that there is a regulation against non-normative households (those of single or divorced women) or that there is an age limit. They

all spoke of the importance of checking people's credit history before approving a loan. However, they did not adequately explain the criteria for checking credibility, saying simply that "it is complicated and confidential." A few agents mentioned that income level and job regularity, along with credit record, were more important than other conditions (such as age or being in a single household); however, these were not mutually exclusive categories.

13. Yun (2005).

14. Homeless women especially bore the brunt of a moralizing discourse in the media, academy, and government policy. The concept of "family breakdown" (*kajŏnghaech'e* or *kajokhaech'e*) signaled a widespread sense of the moral deterioration of woman as domestic caretaker, influencing welfare policy makers and bureaucrats to regard homeless women's issues as insignificant (Song 2006a). For the social impact of the financial crisis in family dynamics, see S-K. Kim and Finch (2002) and Song (2006a).

15. When newspapers proclaimed an increase in domestic violence and runaways, the state did not intervene to provide housing for women in need because women who had left home were not considered to be desirable welfare citizens (Song 2006a, 2009b).

16. See special report by Lee, Pak, and Kim (2009). See also Kim Sang-ch'ŏl (2010); Lim, Sang, and Oh (2009); and Sang and Oh (2009).

17. Travel to the United States is not a viable option for my informants. The United States notoriously restricts the entry of single Korean women because their frustration in Korean society and their desire to emigrate are well-known.

18. As part of the informal sector, the chŏnse market fluctuates with great sensitivity, depending on the regional and national economy. In an interview with a real estate agent in 2012, during work on another research project, I discovered that different methods are used in Busan.

19. The aspiration of home ownership as a desire close to being a lifelong obsession is not a social product limited to Koreans. However, this aspiration can be understood as a historical construction characteristic of the twentieth century, in which one seeks a minimal degree of stability during a time featuring frequent periods of political and economic turbulence. Later in the century, there was increased awareness of the value of ownership as a crucial instrument of a household's upward mobility. It might also be connected to an attachment to land, given that South Korea, as a nation, still holds up the agricultural mode of production as its "authentic" and "traditional" heritage.

20. In Korea, a condominium is called an *apa:t'ŭ*, short for "apartment." Gelézeau (2007), Hôh (2008), and K-Y. Shin (2003) talk about the idiosyncratic appearance and predominance of condominiums as middle- and upper-class living spaces in Korean urban residential areas.

21. The workforce of these big conglomerates comprises 15 percent to 20 percent of the country's total workforce. The conglomerates used to be the symbol of South Korean economic prosperity, the "Miracle of the Han River" (a phrase that went uncontested until the Asian financial crisis, when chaebŏl were held responsible for a ruinous national debt and were subsequently restructured and downsized). See Woo-Cumings (1999) and Eun Mee Kim (1997) in order to understand

the uniqueness of chaebôl in the context of the developing states of Korea and East Asia (in comparison with Japanese conglomerates, *jaibatsu*). There is debate about whether the state was a domineering influence on or was in a more equal partnership with the chaebôl. See also Song (2009b) for the meaning of restructuring chaebôl in the postdevelopment regime, and see J. J. Chun (2009) for the labor process and organization affected by the restructuring.

22. The number of chaebôl has been fluctuating over the last two decades, mainly because of the Asian financial crisis.

23. C. H. Lee, Lee, and Lee (2002) note that Korean chaebôl began to expand their business in financial markets in the domain of nonbank financial institutions in the late 1980s and actively utilized financial markets to supply venture capital during the crisis.

24. I do not want to imply that the developmental state's regulation of banks was necessarily negative or that it invited the Asian financial crisis, preparing the ground for neoliberal intervention. Mainstream economists have attributed the crisis to the South Korean developmental state's planned economy. Nonorthodox economists, such as neo-Keynesian and neo-Ricardian economists, argue that state regulation of the economy in developing countries is necessary to compete with hegemonic, advanced capitalist nation-states in the neoliberal global economy (Chang 2002, 2007; Chang, Chông, and Yi 2005; Crotty and Lee 2001). I take neither of these positions, because even liberal democratic capitalist nation-states have used regulation and intervention, which historically have made up one of the two sides of laissez-faire. Thus, state intervention is not a fundamental tool against neoliberalism but a practical instrument with which to help balance (neo)liberal democracy. See Perelmann (2000) and Song (2009b).

25. A popular TV drama in 2007, *Battlefield of Cash* (*Jjôn ûi chônjaeng*), about the vicious power struggles involved in the usury market, aptly illustrated this process. This drama, and the original graphic novel, are valuable texts. Ethnographic research on the informal loan market is virtually impossible because of the danger of retaliation from gangs linked to usurers. The graphic novel was based on a long-term period of undercover research inside the usurers' society and thus revealed a lot of information unavailable elsewhere (Choi H-y. 2007). In the drama, day loan lenders (*ilsu ôpcha*) are central in informal financial markets. The day loan is actually the common credit method for the wholesale market (*tomae sijang*) and for street business people in old marketplaces such as Dongdaemun Market (see Noritake 2013; Park 2012). The context of the drama is the financial crisis, with its increased demand for informal money lending. Kûm Na-ra, the protagonist, becomes a novice in the usury guild system, the only option available when he must pay back a debt owed by his parents. After struggling to gain the trust of the masters of the usury world, Kûm eventually makes lots of profit by emulating the vicious methods the usurer used on him and his family. These methods remind us of Shakepeare's *The Merchant of Venice*: they entail legal agreements involving bodily liens as security against the debt (*sinche p'ogi kaksô*), such as when Kûm claims the body and life of his debtor's daughter (whom he later marries) as a security deposit. But the drama ends with Kûm being killed on his wedding day. These stories imply that the only way to

succeed is to beat the system at its own game: money making.

26. Following the Asian financial crisis, unregulated banks became more competitive by providing savings accounts with either high interest rates or tax exemptions.

27. What does exist is mostly statistical analysis of the housing market: Dong-chul Cho (2005, 2006), Chang-Moo Lee and Chung (2010), Ambrose and Kim (2003), Kyung-Hwan Kim (2004), Kim and Shin (2011).

28. Nelson's 1991 master's thesis is an exception. Nelson's book (2000), based on her dissertation about gendered public representations of excessive consumption in South Korea, features several pages on Korean housing and the rotating credit system. She is now studying the issue of credit card debt (Nelson 2012). Some eth-nographers working on the subject of women's lives or social networks have noted either chônse or rotating credit associations in passim (Abelmann 2003; Ahn 2009; Kendall 1996; Noritake 2013).

29. See Kim Yongchang (2004), Dongchul Cho (2006), S. Park (2007), K. O. Lee (2007).

30. It is probably for similar reasons that informal loan markets and credit associations have been understudied.

31. A similar system used to be popular throughout Southeast Asia and in Japan. See Geertz (1962) and M. Lee (2005). With regard to kye, see also Campbell and Ahn (1962). Kye is exchangeable with p'umasi as a precapitalist, mutual aid network for agricultural production. However, whereas p'umasi is still known as a social exchange of labor, kye now primarily refers to a relationship that involves regular money transactions, even if some people use kye for the social purpose of a group saving money together so its members can travel together. See Kyung-soo Chun (1984), Kim Chuhûi (1992), and Kwang-Ok Kim (1993). It is also interes-ting to see the ways in which kye is referred to as a popular practice in immigrant communities through Korean Protestant church networks. See Ahn (2009), Kendall (1996, especially p. 29), Oh (2007), Kyeyoung Park (1997, especially p. 187).

32. The current form of kye might be traceable back to Japanese colonialism period, as M. Lee (2005) notes in passing. Also, a Japanese acquaintance from Osaka informed me that there is a similar custom of credit association and chônse among Koreans in the Osaka area, of whom the majority migrated to Japan during the colonial period.

33. Also see Kennedy (1977) for earlier practices of Korean kye.

34. A recent scandal involved a mammoth rotating credit association (kye) called the Association of Multiple Fortunes (tabokhoe), which collapsed in 2008. It was scandalous because of the huge scale of the invested money (presumed to be around 1 trillion won or about $1 billion) and rumors of the involvement of affluent celebrities and members of the social elite (wives of government officials, executives of big corporations, and professors). The scandal demonstrates the popularity and vibrancy of kye activities, even after financial markets were deregulated and legi-timized and credit and investment commodities became readily available. Despite some sympathetic reports on the financial damage inflicted on members of the lower middle class who had blindly joined the association, popular attention focused on

the excessive amount of money that upper class people invested for the purpose of money laundering (or tax evasion). Commenting on the scandal, Kim Sang-jung, the narrator of a well-known TV journalist series, concluded that the Association of Multiple Fortunes invited disaster, not fortunes, because they had tried to earn money through money, not through sweat (that is, through wages from labor). "*Tabokhoe ŭi chinsil keim,*" November 27, 2008.

35. Choi's death also led to the passing of a new civil law on guardianship on April 21, 2011. The existing law automatically transferred the guardianship of any children to the surviving biological parent when the guardian parent died, regardless of domestic violence and abuse records in the past. The new regulation was implemented through the efforts of Choi's fans in the cyber network, who protested the existing law, which transferred the guardianship of Choi's children to her ex-husband, a famous baseball player, who had given up parental rights to his children after his divorce from Choi for repeated domestic violence. The new law on the guardianship screening process is dubbed the "Choi Chin-sil law" (Kim Kyŏng-jin 2011).

36. Nelson (2000) describes the dynamics of a gendered division of labor taken on by the wives of government officials, who were accused of excessive consumption and bribery by (wives of) their husbands' subordinates. While the government could not control kye activities, the condemnation of wives of officials by the media and government targeted these women's links to hidden money flows. Other efforts to grapple with the curb market included tax benefits for people who used their credit/debit cards.

37. See Nancy Abelmann's (2003) study of South Korean middle class, middle-aged women, who compared their life trajectories with those of less successful women siblings and other relatives. See especially the narrative of the Education Mother, a key informant in the book, about her sister, which attributes the sister's failure to her characteristics as unfeminine and unable to quickly figure out benefits (*nunchi ka ôptta*). This demonstrates the gendered expectations imposed on women to be entrepreneurs and to scheme for their family's upward mobility.

38. Although there has been encouragement of domestic consumption since the late 1980s (especially when the export market for expensive commodities, such as automobiles, was limited), there has been persistent public criticism in the media of gendered members of the middle class (wives or mothers of officials) because of their alleged profit making and consumption, activities conducted without their husbands' knowledge. These women's activities include real estate investment (*t'ugi*), large-scale usury (*kûn son*) and heavy involvement in their children's education, either through the facilitation of the private education market (*kwaôe* or *sagyoyuk*) or by bribing school teachers (*ch'imatparam*) (Abelmann 2003; Nelson 2000, 2006; S. J. Park and Abelmann 2004). The way in which women became predominant participants in kye is a historical construct of the postindependence era. Men participated more equally in kye when it functioned along traditional lines of mutual aid. Men made up about 20 percent of kye participants until the 1970s (M. Lee 2005). Compared with the above women's activities, which have negative connotations but are still accepted as prevalent practices and not associated with addiction or criminal activity (to a certain extent), cogendered activities, such as *norûm*

(gambing), *hwatu* (a Korean card game) or *naegi hwatu* (the card game, but with betting for money), and *pokkwôn* (the lottery), are readily associated with addictive and abnormal personalities.

39. Minsô did not pay her father and brother back for the money she needed to rent an apartment. But she considers it to be equivalent to the cost of her wedding or as part of her dowry, which is common logic among the unmarried women I met who borrowed deposit money from their parents and did not feel obliged to pay it back.

40. Maria Mies's classic *Patriarchy and Accumulation* (1986) notes that in South Asia the dowries given by brides' families to bridegrooms' families are *not* a sign of reciprocity and a gift economy *but* a reflection of the sexual hierarchy between men and women, in which the lower status owes tribute to the higher status. It is debatable whether the Korean case of dowry is reciprocal rather than hierarchical because, in the Korean case, both families contribute to the dowry. Although it is convention for the bridegroom (or his family) to provide housing and for the bride (or her family) to provide a dowry that includes furniture, electronics, and utensils, when the bridegroom is a professional, such as a lawyer, prosecutor, medical doctor, or academic professor, the bride's family is expected to provide everything, including housing—often even the workplace for their husbands, such as a doctor's office, or even a whole medical building. This expectation arises in the context of a competitive marriage market and is justified by the allegedly guaranteed income from the groom's job. The situation is similar to what Mies observed in the contemporary Indian marriage market, which also indicates gender hierarchy rather than reciprocity based on equal relations. That said, anthropological concept and literature do not seem to assume that reciprocity and social hierarchy conflict with each other. For example, Marcel Mauss's seminal work *The Gift* (1954) addresses the difference between gift exchange and commodity exchange, presenting cross-cultural indications of gift culture as a way of mediating the social tension that comes primarily from hierarchies within clans, between tribes, and between gods and humans.

41. A similar method of consuming and giving gifts in other East Asian countries is described in Mayfair Yang (1994) and Alan Smart (2003a, 2003b). Smart analyzes the link between the financial and real estate markets. However, there is no research on rents that I am aware of.

42. The manner in which this deposit is invested has shifted since the crisis. These days, it has become common to see affluent landlords putting their savings in banks, because bank interest rates have become competitive with those of informal financial markets, and banks are less risky.

43. Government policy regarding the number of houses or condominiums that can be owned became much more strict over the course of the last two (relatively left-wing) governments (those of Kim Dae Jung, 1998–2003, and Roh Moo Hyun, 2003–2008). Both implemented heavier taxes on people owning more than one or two housing properties. After the experiences of the two previous regimes, the government since then is trying to rescind this kind of taxation.

44. The self-identification of the middle class is subjective. Eighty percent of the population, including heavy industry workers, identified themselves as middle

class in the period running up to the Asian financial crisis, after which the percentage dropped dramatically.

45. Insurance has existed for a long time. In fact, insurance sales have been conducted through the same kinds of social networks as the kye, via married women. What is unique in the postcrisis global financialization period is that insurance clients have expanded to include all age groups, regardless of marital status. See Chagyông, Hosôn, and Haein's insurance stories in this chapter.

46. For example, Nani, in her late thirties, a former private after-school worker harassed by her co-workers for being single, relied on the overdraft available to her on her debit card because she did not want to depend on her family.

47. The way in which disenfranchised people's access to a technology is advertised as providing a means of joining in the circulation of capital is similar to the way in which cell phones and the Internet are introduced through cheap prices into the daily lives of the disenfranchised and the young in South Korea. See S. Yang (2010).

48. The subprime mortgage crisis in the U.S. context is a good example. It happened because of the exposure of the mortgage market to the working poor, as if it were a democratic inclusion. In fact, the crisis was resolved by the working poor facing the financial liability, losing their houses and their livelihoods. In short, the speculative aspect of financial capital cannot but lead to a bubble economy by devaluing other value/asset-building processes. See note 4 in this chapter.

49. The Seoul City public housing development (Shift) demonstrated that the priority for tax fund distribution and government projects is not redistribution or to help poor people.

Chapter 3

1. The liberal ethos itself makes the self or individual a commodity in the labor market (Hindess 2004, Perelman 2000, Read 2001). However, the neoliberal ethos exploits every aspect of the self as a marketable or market-centered component (Guala 2006; Lemke 2001, 2002; Seo 2009; Song 2007).

2. In explaining "technologies of the self," Foucault notes the way his studies of "rules, duties, and prohibitions of sexuality" are involved "not simply with the acts that were permitted and forbidden but with the feelings represented, the thoughts, the desires one might experience, the drives to seek within the self *any hidden feeling, any movement of the soul*, any desire disguised under illusory forms" (1988, 16; italics added).

3. Žižek conceptualizes enjoyment as the fundamental ideology that organizes contradictory and complicated elements of materiality by allowing the subject small transgressions but at the same time leads the subject to conform to the fundamentals of the given capitalist condition (Dean 2006, 190–92).

4. This masculinity-centered culture is argued to have been a result of constructing a militant resistance against the draconian oppression of the military coup-led capitalist state (I. Kwon 2001; S. Moon 2005; Nam 2009).

5. Not all of Chagyông, Tojin, and Sônu's siblings were active in student movements, partly because not all could afford to go to college and partly because not all were interested in participating in them.

6. The cell is the basic training unit in the student movements. According to Sônu, it usually consists of a senior trainer and two junior trainees, usually of the same gender, in order to "avoid sexual intimacy."

7. Other research participants also noted the disparity between the leftist movement in Seoul and non-Seoul areas in terms of women's consciousness.

8. "Partnership between government organizations (GOs) and NGOs" (*minkwan hyômnyôk*) emerged as a quintessential catchphrase that the Kim Dae Jung presidency promoted in response to the Asian financial crisis by inviting grassroots organizations to mitigate economic and social distress through newly launched public works programs. However, rather than becoming "partners" with the state, grassroots organizations and activists became "surrogate" social engineers, the "outsourced" implementers of neoliberal policies on homelessness, unemployment, and gender and family politics. See Song (2009b, 2011) for more detail.

9. The Korean state's participation in the U.S. intervention in the Middle East brought several tragic incidents to Korean civilians. See Han's (2010) piece on Korean missionaries in the Middle East and Africa.

10. See Mun Young Cho (2013) for corporate programs targeting university students who want to experience life abroad.

11. I wonder what my research participants thought about my situation. I am living in one of their ideal locations, so they might have associated me with those people who are extremely fortunate. However, it is notable that they did not ask me about my life in Canada as a legally unmarried person. They might have thought I was in a very different position from them because I am a little older than they are and they did not know about my relatively short immigration history.

12. Ham In-Hui said the word "contrasexual" originated in the United Kingdom. See the *Kontûraseksyôl kwa Han'guksahoe* (Contrasexual and Korean Society) website, http://www.donga.com/fbin/output?sfrm=1&n=200502010340. The heterosexual counterparts of contrasexual women are metrosexual men, who are less masculinist and more stylish single urban professionals.

13. Produced by Choi Pyông-ryun, directed by Yu Hyôn, and written by Han Suk-cha. August 18, 2007.

14. These stereotypes are not just noticeable in the media. Korean government research reports that a focus on the increased number of single households also tends to ignore the population of single people who are not affluent. See Pyôn, Sin, and Cho (2008).

15. Refer to note 21 in chapter 1. See also Oh, August 14, 2009; Cho M-O. (2009) and Jang T-s. (2009).

16. Paeksu literally means "white hand," referring to an idle, lazy worker. The Japanese "freeter" (*frita*) refers to a similar phenomenon (Arai 2005, Muraki 2007). See Song (2009b) for more information.

17. For example, see Kim Chun-il and Im (2007) and also Rah (2005).

18. The Cognitive Style Inventory, a brief introduction to the MBTI, may be obtained in English at http://www.personalitypathways.com/type_inventory.html (accessed May 30, 2013) and in Korean at http://www.assesta.com/images/pdf/ASSES-TA%20카다로그.pdf (accessed May 19, 2010). Sponsored by the Korean Psychological Test Institute (KPTI). An example of NGOs' and NPOs' endorsement of this

program may be found at http://www.icccej.org/bbs/board.php?bo_table=free&wr_id=4239&page=6 (in Korean; accessed May 19, 2010).

19. Available in Korean at http://www.enneagram.co.kr/ (accessed May 19, 2010) and in English at http://www.enneagraminstitute.com/ (accessed May 30, 2013). Both MBTI and Enneagram are actively used to identify children's school performance and career potential (see Wagele 2001). For information about the MBTI used for children, see Kim Ch'ông-yôn (2008).

20. Chagyông ascribed the reason for a woman friend's unsuccessful job experience as a part-time teacher in the same private after-school institute where Chagyông works to her friend's inability to adapt to the intense pressure to elevate students' school performance. Chagyông's boss also held that profitability through intensified work performance was more important than a good personality in the after-school institute market. Her boss was a former male student activist, one of few who survived in the self-employed job market doing jobs such as tutoring, teaching in after-school institutes, marketing (for example, Amway), insurance sales, and working in small independent presses or printing businesses. To my question of how her boss maintained his identity as a leftist intellectual, Chagyông cynically answered, "He donates a lot [to leftist movements] to compensate. He still wants to be part of distributive social justice, but he doesn't want it to upset the process of making profits."

Chapter 4

1. I use the term "lateral agents," inspired by Berlant's notion of "lateral agency" (2007b). See my explanation of this meaning in the following pages.

2. It is hard to say whether her poetry can be read as "feminist" or not. Marxist feminism that maintains a focus on class was predominant during the period in which Ch'oe was actively writing poems. However, despite her criticism of capitalism and the totalitarian nation-state, Ch'oe's addressing of a woman does not appear to be a feminist gesture.

3. She was the first woman to publish in the elite intellectual press. The Korean publisher was Munhak kwa chisông sa (Literature and Intellect).

4. Subaltern propaganda songs (minjung kayo) worked in a similar way.

5. Underground study groups were a popular format for the (re)production of critical intellectuals on university campuses and in night schools for workers, despite the fact that they were spied on by police forces during the military dictatorships. See M. Park (2005) and N. Lee (2005, 2007).

6. Choi's full interview with Kim is published elsewhere (Don Mee Choi 2003).

7. I thank Bonnie McElhinny for reminding me of this point.

8. See Tangherlini (1998), Kwant-Ok Kim (1994), and N. Lee (2007) for more about the indigenous music and dancing culture welcomed by the minjung movement and student activists.

9. I describe a similar passion for TV drama in chapter 3.

10. My research participants, both straight and queer-identified women, noted the cross-dresser's charm. There is an increasing number of graphic novels and comic

books in South Korea in which there are characters of non-normative gender and sexuality.

11. *Suda* (gossip among women) is usually a derogatory way of describing talkative women's chat.

12. In fact, the hopefulness might be näive optimism that reproduces the gloomy status quo—as Berlant labeled it, "cruel optimism" (Berlant 2007a, 2007b).

13. See Song (forthcoming) for ongoing state projects that create mass temporary jobs in tune with gendered care labor.

14. In thinking through the idea of affective labor, I draw upon two further scholarly traditions. One is the longstanding feminist study of care work, emotional labor, and domestic work (Ahmed 2004; Berlant 1998, 2004; Povinelli 2006; Stewart 2007). The other is the popular notion of "immaterial labor" articulated within Italian Marxist literature to describe labor conditioned by the service sector–centered post-Fordist mode of production, which features the growing significance of information and communication technology (Hart and Negri 2004; Lazzarato 1996; Virno 2004). Most Italian Marxists focus on "immaterial labor," without using the concept of "affective labor" and without considering the long feminist tradition of studying emotional labor as immaterial labor.

15. See Introduction for the context of the social panic over the low birth rate.

16. Government and researchers tend to use comparison with other advanced countries to focus on the rapid increase in infertility in Korea. However, this statistic hides the fact that the percentage of Korean women who do not participate in the labor of childbearing and/or child raising (not just single women but also married women without children) is far smaller than in other advanced nations. Other OECD countries' models could be redirected to loosen the pressure on women to participate in reproductive labor. The women's movement has already begun demanding state enhancement of day-care centers for working mothers. It could offer other countries' examples of housing and lending policies that are open to anyone, regardless of age or marriage status.

17. Another example of the coalescing of these different affective domains would be the mass grieving after the death of former president Roh Moo Hyun (Seo Dongjin, personal communication, May 30, 2009). Journalistic reports are found in Yi Chong-sô (2009) and Choi Kwan-ûn (2009).

18. The Candlelight Vigil Demonstration took place every evening from May 24, 2008, to July 18, 2008. In July, it continued as a weekly demonstration and slowly disintegrated in the fall and winter. The first two months of the demonstration were celebrated peacefully by both rally participants and the police. However, beginning in June 2008, and especially on June 10, the twentieth anniversary of a historic demonstration to end the dictatorship, the police began violent suppression of the demonstrators, firing water cannons and beating them with metal pipes. Many people were arrested, including political activists, celebrities, and students who were using cell phones to spread the word. Some cases were brought before the Korean Human Rights Commission, which recognized some human rights violations. The Lee regime later changed the Human Rights Commission leadership to right-wing conservatives. Thus, in a way, the demonstration reaffirmed state repression. However, my focus here is on the earlier stages of the demonstration to highlight its tacit meaning and potential.

19. Although most reports and writing about the Candlelight Vigil Demonstration featured married women, single women (pihon yôsông) participated collectively. See the posters for the single women's rally against discrimination of social minorities within the Candlelight Vigil Demonstration on June 21, 2008, "Ch'abyôl e pandae hanûn haengdong: pihon yôsông haengjin" [Actions against discrimination: single women's rally], at http://cafe.naver.com/equalchrist.cafe?iframe_url=/Article-Read.nhn%3Farticleid=318 (accessed June 9, 2010).

20. The lyrics of "Morning Dew" are very symbolic, and the melody is light and popular. It is a song composed in the 1970s, before political activism against the oppressive military state became militant. Not all songs sung by activists are propaganda, especially those composed after democratization. However, songs composed in the 1980s to mobilize collective resistance, such as Owôl ûi norae (Song of May) and Kû nal i omyôn (If the Day Comes), are solemn and provoking.

21. Tangdaebipyông (2008, 2009), Kyunghyang Sinmun Special Report Team (2008). See also U-Chang Kim 2008, N-C. Yi 2008, and Pressian Book Editorial Board (2008).

22. See Yi Tae-hûi (2008) and Yi Tae-yông (2009).

23. U (2009), notes that the Candlelight Vigil was an example of the younger generation's resistance to the neoliberal job market, labeling it the "quiet revolution."

24. The term sam p'al yuk sedae is not rigid: my research participants who were born in the early 1970s and went to university until the early 1990s can also share the identification.

25. The Introduction to this book and Song (2009b) provide examples of this criticism.

Glossary of Korean Words

Achim isûl: "Morning Dew," a popular Korean song, 아침 이슬
apa:t'û: short for "apartment," which refers to a condominium, 아파트
am pohôm: health insurance that specializes in cancer, 암 보험
arûbaitû: tutor, 아르바이트

Bogeumjari chutaek [Pogûmjari chutaek]: "nest housing," a kind of public housing planned by the Korean government, 보금자리 주택

chaebôl: big conglomerates or big corporations, 재벌
chaetekû: financial know-how or financial techniques, 재테크
chagi kûngjông: self-affirmations, 자기 긍정
chagi kwal'li: self-management, 자기관리
chagi kyebal: self-cultivation, 자기계발
chagi kyebal kangbakchûng: obsession with self-development, 자기계발 강박증
chal môk ko chal sa nûn kô: eat well and live well, 잘 먹고 잘 살는 거
Chamyôyôndae: People's Solidarity for Participatory Democratization, 참여연대
chasusông'ga: build their own lives from scratch, 자수성가
chibang haksaeng: students from the countryside, 지방학생
Chinboyôndae: People's Solidarity for Social Progress, 진보연대
chôchulsan koryônghwa: low fertility and aging society, 저출산 고령화
chongjatton: seed money, 종자돈
chongsin pohôm: life insurance 종신보험

chôngsang chôk iji anta: deviant 정상적이지 않다

chônse: Korean rent system, the predominant rental system of the yearly lease 전세

chônwôlse: combination of a yearly lease and monthly rent, 전월세

chubyônin: close neighbors, which means, literally, people existing in one's surroundings, 주변인

chuche sasang: sovereignty ideology, 주체사상

chutaek ch'ôngyak kwôn: bidding right on new condominiums, 주택청약권

chutaek ch'ôngyak yegûm: savings account specifically for housing, 주택청약예금

chutaek kongsa: state-affilated housing construction company, 주택공사

chutaek tambo taechul: housing loan program, 주택담보대출

ch'abi chôngdo: pocket money for public transportation, 차비 정도

ch'imatparam: bribing school teachers, 치맛바람

ch'ong in'gu chosa: national total population census, 총인구조사

haja ka in nûn: defective, 하자가 있는

hakwon kangsa: teacher in private after-school institute, 학원강사

hojuje: family headship system, 호주제

hojuje p'yeji undong: movement for the removal of the family headship system, 호주제 폐지운동

hongdûng ka: red-light district, 홍등가

hwaryô han sing'gûl ira pul'lô tao: consider me a hip-single, 화려한 싱글이라고 불러다오

hwatu: Korean playing cards adopted from Japan in the late Chosôn dynasty, a popular gambling tool when it involves money or assets (*naegi hwatu*), 화투 (내기화투)

iban yôsông: queer-identified women, 이반여성

ilsu ôpcha: day loan lender, 일수업자

kajok haeche: family breakdown, 가족해체

kajok tôen tori: the way the family does things, 가족된 도리

kajông haech'e: family breakdown, 가정해체

kangje chôk kajokchuûi: coercive familialism, 강제적 가족주의

koldû misû: "golden miss," a label for single women who are seen as too successful and affluent to find a partner, 골드미스

kong'gong imdae chutaek: state-leased affordable condominiums, 공공임대주택

koridaegûm: usury, 고리대금

kosibang: a commercial boarding house for people who are preparing to write national exams, 고시방

kûn son: large-scale usurer, 큰손

Kû nal i omyôn: "If the Day Comes," a Korean propaganda song for subalterns, 그날이 오면

kûnyang nun ttak kam ko salmyô nûn: just live (by getting married to a man) without thinking about the aftermath, 그냥 눈 딱감고 살며는

kwaôe: private education, 과외

kye: rotating credit associations or informal credit association, 계

kyeju: organizer of rotating credit association, 계주

kyôlhon chôngnyông'gi: marriage age, 결혼 적령기

kyôngje kwan'nyôm: an understanding of the economy, 경제관념

kyôngjosa: gifts for celebration and condolence, 경조사

lejûbiôn: lesbian 레즈비언

maei chi an nun salm: free from tied-down life or flexible lifestyle, 매이지 않는 삶

mainôs t'ongjang: minus account, 마이너스 통장

matsôn: date to find a marriage partner arranged by matchmaker, 맞선

mihon: not yet married, 미혼

mihon yôsông: not yet married women, 미혼여성

min'guan hyômnyôk: partnership between government organizations (GOs) and NGOs, 민관협력

minjung: Korean subaltern, 민중

minjung kayo: propaganda songs for subalterns, 민중가요

Minjunochong: Korean Confederation of Trade Unions, 민주노총

moktton: lump-sum money, 목돈

Munhak kwa chisông sa: Literature and Intellect, the name of a publisher specializing in high-brow publications, 문학과 지성사

myôngye namsông: honorary man, 명예 남성

nagayo ch'on: residential village of bar hostesses, 나가요 촌

nakch'al kye: rotating credit by bidding highest interest among members or kye by auction, 낙찰계

ni ka tô pulssang hada: you are more pitiful, 니가 더 불쌍하다

nodongja taetujaeng: the Great Labor Struggle of 1987, the largest labor protest since 1945, 노동자 대투쟁

nohu: when people get old, 노후"

nohu kôkjjông: concern about elderly years, 노후걱정

nohu taechaek: plan for elderly years or a solution for securing elderly years, 노후대책

nunchi ka ôptta: not quick at figuring out benefits, 눈치가 없다

nun'nopi rûl natuô ya: looking for a more humble job or marriage partner, 눈높이를 낮춰야

norûm: gambling, 노름

ohodamdangje: North Korea's rank-and-file five-person units, 오호담당제
Ôn'nine dot.com: a young generation feminist portal site, 언니네 닷컴
Onûl ûi chag'ga sang: Today's Writer, a literary competition, 오늘의 작가 상
opisûtel: office-tel, a building with both offices and hotel rooms, 오피스텔
Owôl ûi norae: "Song of May," a popular propaganda song for subalterns,
    오월의 노래

paeksu: underemployed young adults labeled as good-for-nothings; literally
    means "white hand," referring to an idle, lazy person, 백수
paeryôha nûn taesa: caring narratives, 배려하는 대사
pandong seryôk: force undermining students' activism, 반동세력
pansanghoe: monthly neighborhood meeting, 반상회
pihon: unassociated with marriage, 비혼
pihon yôsông: unmarried women who do not associate with marriage, 비혼
    여성
pit to chasan i ta: a debt can also be an asset, 빚도 자산이다
pojûng'gûm: money for rent deposit, 보증금
pokttôkppang: real estate agency in old style, 복덕방
pudongsan chung'gaeso: real estate agency, 부동산 중개소
puinbyông: women's diseases, 부인병
puôngi hyông in'gan: night-owl people, 부엉이형 인간
pûrimiôm: premium, 프리미엄
p'umasi: precapitalist mutual aid network for agricultural means of produc-
    tion, 품앗이
p'ungmulpae: Korean folk-music bands, 풍물패

sachae: informal loan, 사채
sachae ôp: informal loan business or usury, 사채업
Saeromaji pûl'laen: "New anticipation plan" for low fertility and aging society,
    새로 마지 플랜
sagyoyuk: private education, 사교육
sahoe chôk iljjari: social employment, 사회적 일자리
sahoe chôk kiôp: social enterprise, 사회적 기업
sahoe chôkûng: adjust to social life, 사회적응
sam p'al yuk sedae: "generation of 386," referring to former student activists
    in their thirties (3) who attended universities in the 1980s (8) and were
    born in the 1960s (6), 삼팔육 세대, or 386 세대
samuguan: state official of a certain level, 사무관
silsuyoja: actual demand group, 실수요자
simin sahoe undong: civil society movement, 시민사회운동

sinche p'ogi kaksô: legal agreement to yield part of (or even the whole) body as a security against the debt, 신체포기각서

Siputû: Shift, new public rental housing for the long term, developed by Seoul City and the public housing company, 시프트

sông chôk anjôn sông: sexual safety, 성적 안전성

ssi to an môkil kôt kat ta: they wouldn't take it seriously, no way; literally means "even a seed would not be accepted, not to mention a full plant or tree," 씨도 안 먹힐 것 같다

suda rûl ttô nûn kô: busy chatting, 수다를 떠는 거

sunbôn kye: rotating credit in order of randomly chosen numbers, 순번계

sunjông manhwa: melodramatic graphic novel, 순정만화

sunwûi: priority or hierarchy in bidding, 순위

tabokhoe: Association of Multiple Fortunes, 다복회

tandok chutaek: detached house, 단독주택

tandok sedae: single person's household, 단독세대

taechaek i ôpsôtta: having lived without a plan, 대책이 없었다

toenjang nyô: soybean women—a hostile term for young unmarried women who consume expensive commodities by depending on parents or boyfriends, 된장녀

toksin yôsông: never-married women, 독신여성

toksôsil: private studying rooms for students, 독서실

tolbom sahoe: caring society, 돌봄사회

tomae sijang: wholesale market, 도매시장

tongnip haesô sal myôn wûihôm hada: dangerous to live alone, 독립해서 살면 위험하다

tongsamuso: municipal residential administration or ward office, 동사무소

t'ugi: real estate investment, 투기

undongkwon kayo: propaganda-styled songs for subalterns, 운동권 가요

wôlse: monthly rent, 월세

yôsông: women, 여성

yôsông chônyong imdae chutaek: women-only state-leased affordable condominium, 여성전용임대주택

yôsông kajang: (middle-aged) women who are the head of the family, 여성가장

Glossary of Romanized Korean Books and Films

Ach'im hyŏng in'gan: Morning-Style Person, a translated self-help book, 아침형 인간

Berûsaiyu ûi changmi: Rose of Versailles, a graphic novel, 베르사이유의 장미

Chagi man ûi pang: A Room of One's Own, an essay, 자기만의 방

Chosŏn yŏhyŏngsa Tamo: Tamo, A Woman Cop in the Chosŏn Dynasty, a TV drama, 조선여형사 다모

Jjŏn ûi chŏnjaeng: Battlefield of Cash, a TV drama, 쩐의 전쟁

Kaendi: Candy Candy, a graphic novel, 캔디

Kŏjinmal: Lies, a TV drama, 거짓말

Kajok iyagi: Family Stories, a film, 가족 이야기

K'ŏpi p'ûrinsû ilho chŏm: Coffee Prince Branch Number One, a TV drama, 커피프린스 일호점

Kyŏlhon hago sipûn yŏja: Women Wanting to Get Married, at TV drama, 결혼하고 싶은 여자

Kyŏlhon ûn mich'in chisi ta: Marriage Is Insane, a film, 결혼은 미친짓이다

Masimelo iyagi: Don't Eat the Marshmallow Yet, a translated self-help book, 마시멜로 이야기

Moraesigye: Sandglass, a TV drama, 모래시계

Na, tongnip han ta: Myself, I am going to live independently, an essay collection, 나 독립한다

Nuga nae ch'ijû rûl omgyŏtsûlkka?: Who Moved My Cheese? A translated self-help book, 누가 내 치즈를 옮겼을까?

Oldû misû daiôri: Old Miss Diary, a TV drama, 올드미스 다이어리

Ôn'nine pang I and II: Sister's Room, parts 1 and 2, an essay collection, 언니네 방 I and II

121

Paeksu saenghwal paeksô: Everything about a Good-for-Nothing, a novel, 백수생활백서

Param nan kajok: Family in Affairs, a film, 바람난 가족

Puja appa kanan han appa: Rich Dad Poor Dad, a translated self-help book, 부자아빠 가난한 아빠

Pulkkot: Flare, a TV drama, 불꽃

Sing'gûl ira to kwaenchan a: It Is Fine for a Woman to Be Single, a TV documentary produced by Munhwa Broadcasting Company (MBC), 싱글이라도 괜찮아

Sing'gûljû: Singles, a film, 싱글즈

Sôngkong ha nûn saram tûl ûi ilgopkaji sûpkwan: The Seven Habits of Highly Effective People, a translated self-help book, 성공하는 사람들의 일곱 가지 습관

Sôyang koldong yang'guaja chôm: Western Antique Cookie Shop, a graphic novel, 서양골동양과자점"

Tabokhoe ûi chinsil keim: Truth or Dare in a rotating credit association, a TV documentary, 다복회의 진실게임

Taejang'gûm: A Jewel in the Palace, a TV drama, 대장금

Toksin ch'ônha: Singles' World, a TV drama, 독신천하

List of Research Participants' Pseudonyms

Chagyông: A private school teacher who inherited public housing from her late mother; in her late thirties.

Chisu: A relatively well-paid private school teacher who moved out from her parents' home but still lives in the same city; in her mid-thirties.

Chunhee: a former office worker who moved out from her parents' home with the excuse that she was going to a university in a different city. Once she ran away from her parents. In her early thirties.

Haein: Working in the secondary financial market with the catchphrase "high risk, high return"; living in an office-tel; in her mid-thirties.

Hosôn: Between jobs. Bravely moved out from her parents' home without any excuse. In her late thirties.

Kyuri: A working-poor–class woman who explicitly spoke of poverty or marriage as the only options for unmarried women; in her mid-thirties.

Minsô: Happily working in a NGO for minimum wage, having come to live alone after parents went to countryside and brother got married; in her mid-thirties.

Miyông: Graduate student who expressed that living alone is a challenge because of sexual safety; in her mid-thirties.

Nani: Former private education worker who was harassed by coworkers for not being interested in marriage and because she lived alone; in her late thirties.

Pohûi: Eking out a living as a low-paid NGO worker and an insurance salesperson, living alone in her parents' home; in her mid-thirties.

Sojông: A freelance translator who moved out from her parents' home with the excuse that she was going to a university in a different city; in her early thirties.

Sônu: A former student activist whose role in the activism was taking care of new members; in her late thirties.

Tojin: A former worker in a women's movement organization who tried to live in women-only public housing; in her mid-thirties.

Togyông: An NGO worker who loves traveling; in her late thirties.

Wony: A dedicated worker in an NGO; a researcher who paid back half of the lump-sum deposit she had borrowed from her parents; in her late thirties.

Yoon: A former office worker in a small office who makes living by tutoring; in her mid-thirties.

Bibliography

Abelmann, Nancy. 1996. *Echoes of the Past, Epics of Dissent: A South Korean Social Movement*. Berkeley: University of California.

———. 2003. *Melodrama of Mobility: Women, Talk, and Class in Contemporary South Korea*. Honolulu: University of Hawai'i.

Ahmed, Sara. 2004. *The Cultural Politics of Emotion*. Edinburgh: University of Edinburgh.

Ahn, Kyung Ju. 2009. "South Korean Transnational Mothers: Familism, Cultural Criticism and Education Project." PhD diss., University of Syracuse.

Ambrose, Brent W., and Sunwoong Kim. 2003. "Modeling the Korean Chonsei Lease Contract" *Real Estate Economics*. 31(1):53-74.

Arai, Andrea G. 2005. "The Neo-Liberal Subject of Lack and Potential: Developing 'the Frontier within' and Creating a Reserve Army of Labor in 21st Century Japan." *Rhizomes: Cultural Studies in Emerging Knowledge* 10 (Spring). Accessed June 2, 2013. http://www.rhizomes.net/issue10/arai.htm.

Baker, Don. 2009. *Korean spirituality*. Honolulu: University of Hawai'i Press.

Barlow, Tani. 2004. *The Question of Women in Chinese Feminism*. Durham, NC: Duke University Press.

Barraclough, Ruth. 2009. "Slum Romance in Korean Factory Girl Literature." In *Gender and Labour in Korea and Japan*. Edited by R. Barraclough and E. Faison, 60–77. London: Routledge.

Barrow, Christine. 1988. "Anthropology, the Family, and Women in the Caribbean." In *Gender in Caribbean Development*. Edited by Patricia Mohammed and Catherine Shepherd, 156–69. Mona, Jamaica: University of the West Indies Women and Development Studies Project.

Barry, Kathleen. 2007. *Femininity in Flight: A History of Flight Attendants*. Durham, NC: Duke University Press.

Berlant, Lauren, ed. 1998. "Intimacy." Special issue, *Critical Inquiry* 24 (3): 281–88.

————, ed. 2004. *Compassion: The Culture and Politics of an Emotion*. New York: Routledge.

————. 2007a. "Nearly Utopian, Nearly Normal: Post-Fordist Affect in La Promesse and Rosetta." *Public Culture* 19 (2): 273–301.

————. 2007b. "Slow Death (Sovereignty, Obesity, Lateral Agency)." *Critical Inquiry* 33 (4): 754–80.

Bolles, A. Lynn. 1996. *Sister Jamaica: A Study of Women, Work and Households in Kingston*. Lanham, MD: University Press of America.

Bumiller, Kristin. 2008. *In an Abusive State: How Neoliberalism Appropriated the Feminist Movement against Sexual Violence*. Durham, NC: Duke University Press.

Cameron, Julia. 1992. *The Artist's Way: A Spiritual Path to Higher Creativity*. New York: Jeremy P. Tarcher/Putnam.

————. 1997. *Aju t'ŭkpyŏl han chŭlgôum* [A very special pleasure]. Translated by Yi Chông-gi. Seoul: Tajôngwôn.

Campbell, Colin D., and Chang Shick Ahn. 1962. "Kyes and Mujins: Financial Intermediaries in South Korea." *Economic Development and Cultural Change* 11 (1): 55–68.

Chang, Ha-Joon. 2002. *Kicking Away the Ladder*. London: Anthem Press.

————. 2006. *The East Asian Development Experience: The Miracle, the Crisis and the Future*. London: Zed Books.

————. 2007. *Bad Samaritans: Rich Nations, Poor Policies, and the Threat to the Developing World*. London: Random House Business Books.

————, Chông Sông-il, and Yi Chong-t'ae. 2005. *K'waedo nanma han'guk kyôngje* [Trenchant analysis of difficult Korean economy]. Seoul: Puki Press.

Chatterjee, Partha. 2011. *Lineages of Political Society: Studies in Postcolonial Democracy*. New York: Columbia University Press.

Cheng, Sea-Ling. 2002. "Changing Lives, Changing Selves: 'Trafficked' Filipina Entertainers in Korea." *Anthropology in Action* 9 (1): 13–20.

————. 2005. "Popularizing Purity: Gender, Sexuality, Nationalism in HIV/AIDS Prevention for South Korean Youths. *Asia Pacific Viewpoint* 46 (1): 7–20.

Cho, Dongchul. 2005. "Interest Rate, Inflation, and Housing Price: With an Emphasis on Chonsei Price in Korea." Working Paper 11054. Cambridge, MA: National Bureau of Economic Research. Available at http://www.nber.org/papers/w11054.

————. 2006. "Interest Rate, Inflation, and Housing Price: With an Emphasis on Chonsei Price in Korea. In *Monetary Policy with Very Low Inflation in the Pacific Rim*. Edited by Takatoshi Ito and Andrew K. Rose, 341–70. Chicago: University of Chicago Press.

Cho Hyông, ed. 1996. *Yangsông pyôngdŭng kwa Han'guk pyôp ch'egye* [Gender Equality and South Korean Law System]. Seoul: Ehwa Woman's University Press.

Cho Mun-Ok. 2009. "*Kŭinong ŭro che 2 ŭi salmŭl sôlgye hada*" [Planning the second life by returning to farming life]. *Cheju ilbo*, local section, August 13. Accessed June 9, 2010. http://www.jejunews.com/news/articleView.html?idxno=375022#.

Cho, Mun Young. 2013. "*Kong'gong ira nŭn irŭm ŭi ch'iyu: Han tae kiôp ŭi haeoe chawôn pongsa hwaldong ŭl t'ong hae pon Han'guk sahoe 'pan pin'gon' kwa 'tae-haksaeng' ŭi chihyôngdo*" [Healing in the name of the public: A South Korean topography of "antipoverty" and "university student" through a volunteer activity program abroad, sponsored by a big conglomerate]. *Han'guk munhwa illyuhak* [Korean cultural anthropology] 46 (2): 45–91.

Cho, Sang-Wook Stanley. 2009. "Household Wealth Accumulation and Portfolio Choices in Korea." *Journal of Housing Economics* 19 (1): 13–25.

Cho, Sun-Kyung. 1999. *Yŏsŏnghaego ŭi silt'ae wa chŏngch'aek kwaje* [Women's lay-off and suggestions for policy making]. Seoul: Presidential Commission on Women's Affairs.

Ch'oe Sŭng-ja. 2006. "For Suk." In *Anxiety of Words*. Translated by D. M. Choi, 56. Brookline, MA: Zephyr Press.

Choi, Don Mee. 2003. "Korean Women—Poetry, Identity, Place: A Conversation with Kim Hye-sun. *Positions: East Asia Cultures Critique* 11 (3): 529–39.

———. 2006. *Anxiety of Words: Contemporary Poetry by Korean women*. Brookline, MA: Zephyr Press.

Choi, Eunyoung. 2010. "Gender, Justice and Geopolitics of Undocumented North Korean Migration." PhD diss., Syracuse University.

Choi Ho-yŏl. 2007. "Jjŏn ŭi chŏnjaeng wonjak manhwaga Pak In-kwŏn ŭi sachae ŏpkye 5nyŏn ch'ehŏm" [Five years of experience in the usurers' world by Pak In-kwon, the author of a comic book, *Battlefield of Cash*]. *Sin Donga* [New Donga], July 6. http://www.donga.com/fbin/output?n=200707060413.

Choi, Hyaeweol. 2009. *Gender and Mission Encounters in Korea: New Women, Old Ways*. Berkeley: University of California Press.

Choi, Kyeong-Hee. 1999. "Neither Colonial nor National: The Making of the New Women in Pak Wanso's 'Mother's Stake 1.'" In *Colonial Modernity in Korea*. Edited by Gi-Wook Shin and Michael Robinson, 221–47. Cambridge, MA: Harvard University Press.

———. 2001. "Impaired Body as Colonial Trope: Kang Kyong'ae's 'Underground Village.'" *Public Culture* 13 (3): 431–58.

Choi Kwang-ûn. 2009. "*Lee Myung Pak chŏngbu ka pŏl in chugŭm ŭi kutpan, ajik kkŭt i ani ta*" [Lee Myung Pak government's ritual for the dead (Roh Moo Hyun) hasn't been done (for other cases)]. *Oh My News*, May 27. Accessed June 9, 2009. http://www.ohmynews.com/NWS_Web/View/at_pg.aspx?CNTN_CD=A0001142234.

Chôn Chin-sik. 2006. "*Yŏnshoe salinbŏm Chŏng ssi wa Yu Yŏng-chôl sagŏn ŭi kyohun*" [Lessons from the serial killers Chŏng and Yu Yŏng-chôl]. *Han'gyŏre*, April 27. Accessed June 8, 2010. http://www.hani.co.kr/arti/society/society_general/119158.html.

Choo, Hae Yeon. 2013. "The Cost of Rights: Migrant Women, Feminist Advocacy, and Gendered Morality in South Korea." *Gender & Society* 27 (4): 445–68.

Chun, Kyung-soo. 1984. *Reciprocity and Korean Society: An Ethnography of Hasami*. Seoul: Seoul National University Press.

Chun, Jennifer Jihye. 2009. *Organizing at the Margins: Labor Politics and Globalization in South Korea and the United States*. Ithaca, NY: Cornell University Press.

Chun, Soonok. 2003. *They Are Not Machines: Korean Women Workers and Their Fight for Democratic Trade Unionism in the 1970s*. Farnham, Surrey: Ashgate.

Chung, Hyun Kyung. 1990. *Struggle to Be the Sun Again: Introducing Asian Women's Theology*. Maryknoll, NY: Orbis Books.

Covey, Stephen. 2004. *The Seven Habits of Highly Effective People* [Sôngkong ha nûn saram tûl ûi ilgopkaji sûpkwan]. Translated by Kim Kyông-sôp. Seoul: Kimyôngsa.

Crotty, James, and Kang-Kook Lee. 2001. "Economic Performance in Post-Crisis Korea: A Critical Perspective on Neoliberal Restructuring." Working Paper Series 64. Amherst: Political Economy Research Institute, University of Massachusetts.

———. 2005a. "The Causes and Consequences of Neoliberal Restructuring in Post-Crisis Korea." In *Financialization and the World Economy*. Edited by Gerald A. Epstein, 334–56. Northampton, MA: Edward Elgar Publishing.

———. 2005b. "From East Asian 'Miracle' to Neo-Liberal 'Mediocrity': The Effects of Liberalization and Financial Opening on the Post-Crisis Korean Economy." *Global Economic Review* 34 (4): 415–34.

Cruikshank, Barbara. 1999. *The Will to Empower: Democratic Citizens and Other Subjects*. Ithaca, NY: Cornell University Press.

Davis, Mike. 2004. "Planet of Slums: Urban Involution and the Informal Proletariat." *New Left Review* 26: 5–34.

Dean, Jody. 2006. *Žižek's Politics*. New York: Routledge.

de Posada, Joachim, and Ellen Singer. 2005. *Don't Eat the Marshmallow Yet: The Secret to Sweet Success in Work and Life* [Masimelo iyagi]. Translated by Kong Kyông-hee. Seoul: 21segi buks.

Deuchler, Martina. 1992. *The Confucian Transformation of Korea: A Study of Society and Ideology*. Cambridge, MA: Harvard University Press.

Dorow, Sara. 2006. *Transnational Adoption: A Cultural Economy of Race, Gender, and Kinship*. New York: New York University Press.

Ducey, Ariel. 2007. "More Than a Job: Meaning, Affect, and Training Health Care Workers." *The Affective Turn: Theorizing the Social*. Edited by Patricia Ticineto Clough, with Jean Halley, 187–208. Durham, NC: Duke University Press.

Eisenstein, Hester. 2009. *Feminism Seduced: How Global Elites Used Women's Labor and Ideas to Exploit the World*. Boulder, CO: Paradigm Publishers.

Eisenstein, Zillah. 2007. *Sexual Decoys: Gender, Race, and War in Imperial Democracy*. Melbourne: Sinifex/Zed Books.

Elyachar, Julia 2010. "Phatic Labor, Infrastructure, and the Question of Empowerment in Cairo." *American Ethnologist* 37(3): 452–64.

———, and Jessica Winegar. 2012. "Revolution and Counter-Revolution in Egypt a Year after January 25th." *Cultural Anthropology Online*. Field Spots–Hot Spots. February 2. Accessed October 19, 2013. http://www.culanth.org/fieldsights/208-revolution-and-counter-revolution-in-egypt-a-year-after-january-25th.

Engels, Friedrich. 1979. *Housing question*. Moscow: Progress Publisher.

Foucault, Michel. 1988. "Technologies of the Self." In *Technologies of the Self: A Seminar with Michel Foucault*. Edited by Luther H. Martin, Huck Gutman, and Patrick H. Hutton, 16–49. Amherst: University of Massachusetts Press.

———. 1998. *Ethics: Subjectivity and Truth*. Essential Works of Foucault 1954–1984, edited by Paul Rabinow. New York: The New Press.

Freeman, Caren. 2011. *Making and Faking Kinship: Marriage and Labor Migration between China and South Korea*. Ithaca, NY: Cornell University Press.

Freeman, Carla. 2000. *High Tech and High Heels in the Global Economy: Women, Work, and Pink-Collar Identities in the Caribbean*. Durham, NC: Duke University Press.

———. 2007. "The 'Reputation' of Neoliberalism." *American Ethnologist* 34 (2): 252–67.

Gage, Sue-je. 2007. "The Amerasian Problem: Blood, Duty, and Race." *International Relations*. 21 (1): 86–102.

Geertz, Clifford. 1962. "The Rotation Credit Association: A Middle Rung in Development." *Economic Development and Cultural Change* 10 (3): 242–63.

Gelézeau, Valérie. 2007. *Apatû konghwaguk: Pûrangsû chirihakcha ka pon han'guk ûi apatû* [Republic of condominium: South Korean condominium examined by French geographer]. Translated by Kil H. Seoul: Humanitasû.

Graeber, David. 2011. *Debt: The First 5,000 Years*. Brooklyn, NY: Melville House.

Guala, Francesco. 2006. Critical Notice: Naissance de la Biopolitique: Cours au Collège de France, 1978–1979, Michel Foucault. *Economics and Philosophy* 22: 429–39.

Haboush, Jahyun Kim. 1991. The Confucianization of Korean Society. In *The East Asian Region: Confucian Heritage and Its Modern Adaptation*. Edited by G. Rozman. Princeton, NJ: Princeton University Press.

Hae, Laam. 1999. "*Ch'unchôn si ch'ukche e nata nan changso maketing ûi sông'gyôk: chamyô chuche kujo wa chuche kan kaldûng kwan'gye rûl chungsim û ro*" [Festivals in Chun-chon and place marketing: conflicts among participating agents]. Master's thesis, Seoul National University, Seoul.

Han, Judy Ju Hui. 2010. "'If You Don't Work, You Don't Eat': Evangelizing Development in Africa." In *New Millennium South Korea: Neoliberal Capitalism and Transnational Movements*. Edited by Jesook Song, 142–58. London: Routledge.

Hart, Keith 2009. "On the Informal Economy: The Political History of an Ethnographic Concept." CEB Working Paper no. 09/042. Université Libre de Bruxelles, Solvay Brussels School of Economics and Management, Centre Emile Bernheim. Accessed June 2, 2013. https://dipot.ulb.ac.be:8443/dspace/bitstream/2013/54329/1/RePEc_sol_wpaper_09-042.pdf.

Hart, Michael, and Antonio Negri. 2004. *Multitude: War and Democracy in the Age of Empire*. New York: Penguin.

Harvey, David. 2005. *A Brief History of Neo-Liberalism*. Oxford: Oxford University Press.

———. [1976] 2007. *The Limits to Capital*. Rev. ed. London: Verso.

———. 2000. "The Body as Accumulation Strategy." In *Spaces of Hope*, 97–116. Berkeley: University of California Press.

Hilferding, Rudolf. 1981. *Finance Capital: A Study of the Latest Phase of Capitalist Development*. London: Routledge and Kegan Paul Ltd.

Hindess, Barry. 2004. "Liberalism: What's in a Name?" In *Global Governmentality: Governing International Spaces*. Edited by Wendy Larner and William Walters, 23–39. London: Routledge.

Ho, Karen. 2009. "Disciplining Investment Bankers, Disciplining the Economy: Wall Street's Institutional Culture of Crisis and the Downsizing of 'Corporate America." *American Anthropologist* 111 (2): 177–89.

Hochschild, Arlie Russell. 1983. *The Managed Heart: Commercialization of Human Feeling.* Berkeley: University of California Press.

Hoffman, Lisa. 2010. *Patriotic Professionalism in Urban China: Fostering Talent.* Philadelphia, PA: Temple University Press.

Hôh Ûi-Do. 2008. *Nangman apatû: uri sidae wihôm han munhwa k'odû ilggi* [Condominium romance: Deciphering the risky cultural code of our time]. Seoul: Planet Media.

Hughes, Theodore. 2011. "Return to the Colonial Present: Ch'oe In-hun's Cold War Pan-Asianism." *positions: east asia cultures critique* 19 (1): 109–31.

———— 2012. *Literature and Film in Cold War South Korea: Freedom's Frontier.* New York: Columbia University Press.

Hulchanski, David. 2007. "Rental Housing: The Ultimate Housing Dilemma." Paper presented at Conference on Transformation in Housing, Urban Life, and Public Policy, Asia Pacific Network for Housing Research, Seoul, South Korea, August 30 to September 1.

———, and Michael Shapcott, eds. 2004. *Finding Room: Policy Options for a Canadian Rental Housing Strategy.* Toronto: University of Toronto Press.

Hwang, Merose. 2009. "The *Mudang*: Gendered Discourses on Shamanism in Colonial Korea." PhD diss., University of Toronto.

Inoue, Miyako. 2006. "What Do Women Want? Gender Equity and the Ethics and Aesthetics of Self in Neoliberal Japan." Paper presented at the annual meetings of the American Anthropological Association, San Jose, CA, November.

Ive, Graham. 1974. "Walker and the 'New Conceptual Framework' of Urban Rent." *Antipode* 7 (1): 20–30.

Janelli, Roger, and Dawnhee Yim. 1988. "Interest Rates and Rationality: Rotation Credit Associations among Seoul Women." *Journal of Korean Studies* 6 (1): 165–91.

Janelli, Roger L., and Dawnhee Yim Janelli. 1982. *Ancestor Worship and Korean society.* Stanford, CA: Stanford University Press.

Jang, Jin-Ho. 2011. "Neoliberalism in South Korea: The Dynamics of Financialization." In *New Millennium South Korea: Neoliberal Capitalism and Transnational Movements.* Edited by Jesook Song, 46–59. London: Routledge.

Jang Tae-sôk. 2009. "*Sin kûinong sidae (sang) 'hûk e salli ra' sigol lo ka nûn 4050*" [New era of returning to farming life: "I'm gonna live in soil." People in their 40s and 50s who go to the countryside]. *Chungang ilbo,* social section, July 25. Accessed July 22, 2013. http://article.joins.com/news/article/article.asp?ctg=12&Total_ID=3700343.

Jessop, Bob. 1994. "The Transition to Post-Fordism and the Schumpeterian Workfare State." In *Towards a Post-Fordist Welfare State?* Edited by Roger Burrows and Brian Loader, 13–37. London: Routledge.

Johnson, Spencer, and Kenneth Blanchard. 2000. *Who Moved My Cheese?* [Nuga nae ch'ijû rûl omgyôtsûlkka?]. Translated by Yi Yông-jin. Seoul: Chinmyông ch'ulpansa.

Jones, Nicola Anne. 2006. *Gender and the Political Opportunities of Democratization in South Korea.* New York: Palgrave Macmillan.

Joo, Rachael. 2012. *Transnational Sport: Gender, Media, and Global Korea.* Durham, NC: Duke University Press.

Joseph, Miranda. 2002. *Against the Romance of Community*. Minneapolis: University of Minnesota Press.

Jun, EuyRyung. 2012. "'We Have to Transform Ourselves First': The Ethics of Liberal Developmentalism and Multicultural Governance in South Korea." *FOCAAL: Journal of Global and Historical Anthropology* 64: 99–112.

Jung, Ji-Young. 2009. "Widows' Position and Agency in the Late Chôson Dynasty." *Journal of Korean Studies* 14(1): 61–82.

Kang Chun-man. 2000. *Saramdûl ûn uae punno rûl irôtsûlgga* [Why did people lose indignation?]. Seoul: Inmul kwa sasangsa.

Kang, Jiyeon. 2012. "Corporeal Memory and the Making of a Post-Ideological Social Movement: Remembering the 2002 South Korean Candlelight Vigils." *Journal of Korean Studies* 17 (2): 329–50.

Keller, Nora Okja. 2003. *Fox Girl*. New York: Penguin.

Kelsky, Karen. 2001. *Women on the Verge: Japanese Women, Western Dreams*. Durham, NC: Duke University Press.

Kendall, Laurel, ed. 1996. *Getting Married in Korea: Of Gender, Morality, and Modernity*. Berkeley: University of California Press.

Kennedy, Gerald F. 1976. "The Korean *Kye*: Maintaining Human Scale in a Modernizing Society." *Korean Studies* 1: 197–222.

Kim Chong-suk, Kim Hye-yông, Kim Nam-ju, and Nam Chae-ryang. 2007. *"Taejol yôsông ch'ôngnyôn ch'ûng nodong sijang kujo pak kwa chôngchaek kwaje"* [Structural analysis and policy suggestions regarding labor market for young adult women with university degrees]. Research report no. 5. Seoul: Han'guk yôsông chôngchaek yôn'guwon [Korean women's development institute].

Kim Ch'ông-yôn. July 13, 2008. *Ai simni kômsa, anûn mankûm hyogwa ponda* [There are more effects when we know more about children's psychology tests]. Accessed May 5, 2010. http://www.hani.co.kr/arti/society/schooling/298565.html.

Kim Chuhûi. 1992. *P'umasi wa Chông ûi In'gan Kwan'gae* [The Human Relations of P'umasi and Chông]. Seoul: Jimmundang.

Kim Chun-il, and Im Hyôn-ju. 2007. *"Puran han chikchangin tûl 'chagi kyebal kangbak chûng'"* [Salaried Men and Women Insecure Due to "impulsive obsession of self-development/improvement"]. *Kyônghyang sinmun*, March 2.

Kim, Eleana. 2010. *Adopted Territory: Transnational, Korean Adoptees, and the Politics of Belonging*. Durham, NC: Duke University Press.

———. 2012. "Human Capital: Transnational Korean Adoptees and the Neoliberal Logic of Return." *Journal of Korean Studies* 17(2): 299–327.

Kim, Eun Mee. 1997. *Big Business, Strong State: Collusion and Conflict in South Korean Development, 1960–1990*. Albany: State Universty of New York Press.

Kim Hûi-su, Yun-ha, Jang-mi, Yi Sûng-min, Suk-kyông, KwonJông Yôn-su, Yi Ok-im, and Chông Hûi-sôn. 2007. *Na, tongnip han ta* [I am going to live independently]. Seoul: Ilda Press.

Kim Hyôn-jin. 2009. *Kûraedo ôn'ni nûn kan ta: aeng'gûri yông gôl ûi Yi Myung-Bak sidae saranamggi* [Nonetheless, sister is coming: Angry young woman's survival of Yi Myung-Bak regime]. Seoul: Kaemagowôn.

Kim Hyun Mee. 2000. "Han'guk ûi kûndaesông kwa yôsông ûi nodongkwôn" [Modernity and women's labor rights in South Korea]. *Yôsônghak nonjip* [Journal of Korean women's studies] 16 (1): 37–64.

Kim, Janice C. H. 2009. *To Live to Work: Faculty Women in Colonial Korea 1910–1945*. Stanford, CA: Stanford University Press.

Kim Ki-hwan. 2011. *"Haeôi ro kan sain ûi ch'uiôp sông'gong ki"* [Four success stories of employment abroad]. *Chungang kyôngje*, April 22, E2.

Kim, Kwant-Ok. 1993. "The Religious Life of the Urban Middle Class." *Korea Journal* 33 (4): 5–33.

_____1994. "Rituals of Resistance: The Manipulation of Shamanism in Contemporary Korea. In *Asian Visions of Authority*. Edited by Charles F. Keyes, Laurel Kendall, and Helen Hardacre, 195–220. Honolulu: University of Hawai'i Press.

Kim Kyông-jin. 2011. *"Pujôk'kyôk ch'in'ggônja pôpwôn i maknûn ta"* [Court regulates irrelevant parents from guardianship transfer]. *Chungang ilbo*, society section, April 22, 18.

Kim, Kyounghee. 2009.*"Sôngbyôlhwa toen chôimgûm tolbomnodong ûi chaesaengsan kwuajông yôn'gu: pigongsik pumun ûi tolbomnodong ûl chungsim ûro"* [A Study on the Reproduction Process of Gendered and Low-Wage Care Workers: Focused on Care Work in the Informal Sector]. *Asia yôsông yôn'gu* [Journal of Asian women] 48 (2): 147–84.

Kim, Kyung-Hwan. 2004. "Housing and the Korean Economy." *Journal of Housing Economics* 13 (4): 321–41.

Kim, Minjeong. 2008. "Gendering Marriage Migration and Fragmented Citizenship Formation: 'Korean' Wives, Daughters-in-Law, and Mothers from the Philippines." PhD diss., University of Albany, State University of New York.

Kim Sang-ch'ôl. 2010. *"Imdae mulnyang ûl chungsanch'ûng chutaek ûro pakun ke sipûtû"* [Rent apartment changed to middle class condominium, that is Shift]. *Han'gyôre*, April 14. Accessed May 11, 2010. http://www.hani.co.kr/arti/opinion/readercolumn/416036.html.

Kim, Se-Jik, and Hyun Song Shin. 2011. "Financing Growth without Banks: Korean Housing Repo Contract." Princeton University: Hyun Song Shin. Accessed October 20, 2013. http://www.princeton.edu/~hsshin/www/housingrepo.pdf.

Kim, Seung-Kyung. 1997. *Class Struggle or Family Struggle? The Lives of Women Factory Workers in South Korea*. Cambridge: Cambridge University Press.

Kim, Seung-Kyung, and John Finch. 2002. "Living with Rhetoric, Living against Rhetoric: Korean Families and the IMF Economic Crisis. *Korean Studies* 26 (1): 120–39.

Kim Su-jin. 2009. *Sin yôsông: kûndae ûi kwaing* [New women: Excess of modernity]. Seoul: Somyông.

Kim Sun-yông. 2011. *Taech'ul kuôn ha nûn sahôe* [Society that encourage credit]. Seoul: Humanitas.

Kim, U-Chang. 2008 *"Chôngûi wa chôngûi ûi chogôn: chôngûi roun in'gan chilsô e tae han myôtkkaji saenggak"* [Justice and condition of justice: a few thoughts on human order of justice]. *Kyegan pipyông* [Critique quarterly], no. 20 (Fall): 11–90.

Kim Yongchang. 2004. *Han'guk ûi t'oji chutaekchôngchaek* [South Korea's real estate and housing policy]. Seoul: Puyônsa.

Kim Yông-Sôn. 2007. *"Ch'abyôl kûmji pôp esô ppajin haeksim chohang tûl: In'gwôn wûi kwôn'go pôban kwa muôt i talla chônna?"* [Key items excluded from discrimination inhibition law: What has changed from the previous human rights recommendations?]. *Yôsôngjuûi chônôl ilda* [Feminist Journal Ilda], November 9, 2007. Accessed June 23, 2010. http://www.ildaro.com/sub_read.html?uid=4 128&section=sc1&section2=%C0%CF%B9%DD.

Kittay, E. F. 1999. *Love's Labor: Essays on Women, Equality, and Dependency*. New York: Routledge.

Kiyosaki, Robert. 2000. *Rich Dad, Poor Dad* [Puja appa kanan han appa]. Translated by An Chin-hwan. Seoul: Hwang'gûmgaji.

Koo, Hagen. 2001. *Korean Workers: The Culture and Politics of Class Formation*. Ithaca, NY: Cornell University.

Korea Statistics Promotion Institute. 2010. *2005 chôn'guk song pyôl/yôllyông pyôl/ chômyu hyôngtae pyôl/hon'in sangtae pyôl ilin kagu*. [2005 statistics report on single households with multiple variables by gender, age, residential types, and marriage status]. Seoul: Korea Statistics Promotion Institute.

Kwon, Insook. 2001. "Feminist Exploration of Military Conscription: The Gendering of the Connections between Nationalism, Militarism and Citizenship in South Korea." *International Feminist Journal of Politics* 3(1): 26–54.

Kwon, June Hee. 2003. "Mobile Ethnicity: The Formation of the Korean Chinese Transnational Migrant Class." PhD diss., Duke University.

Kwon Myông-ah. 2012. *Muhanhi chôngch'i chôk in ôiroum* [Boundless political solitude]. Seoul: Kalmuri.

Kwôn Kyông-hûi and Im Tong-sun. 2011. *Tu yôja wa tu nyangi ûi kûich'on ilgi* [Diary of returning to farming by two women and two cats]. Seoul: Ilda.

Kyunghyang Sinmun Special Report Team. 2008. *Minjuhwa 20 nyôn, chisikin ûi chugûm, chisikin, kûdûl ûn ôdi e sô inna?* [Twentieth anniversary of democratization and death of intellectuals: where are they standing now?]. Seoul: Humanitas.

Lafargue, Paul. 1907. *The Right to Be Lazy and Other Studies*. Translated by Charles H. Kerr. Chicago: C. H. Keri.

———. 2005. *Keûrûl su innûn kôlli* [The right to be lazy]. Translated by H. Cho. Seoul: Saemulgyôl.

Langley, Paul. 2008. *Everyday Life of Global Finance: Saving and Borrowing in Anglo-America*. Oxford: Oxford University Press.

Lapavitsas, Costas. 2009. "Financialized Capitalism." *Historical Materialism* 17: 114–48.

Lawson, Victoria. 2007. "Geographies of Care and Responsibility." *Annals of the Association of American Geographers* 97(1): 1–11.

Lazzarato, Maurizio. 1996. "Immaterial Labor." In *Radical Thought in Italy: A Potential Politics*. Edited by Paolo Virno and Michael Hardt, 133–46. Minneapolis: University of Minnesota Press.

Lee, Chang-Moo, and Eui-Chul Chung. 2010. "Monthly Rent with Variable Deposit: A New Form of Rental Contract in Korea." *Journal of Housing Economics* 19 (4): 315–23.

Lee, Chung H., Keun Lee, and Kangkook Lee. 2002. "Chaebols, Financial Liberalization and Economic Crisis: Transformation of Quasi-Internal Organization in Korea." *Journal of Asian Economics* 16 (1): 17–35.

Lee C-W., Pak H. R., and Kim S. C. 2009. *Seoul si kongkong imdae chutaek konggŭk mit kwalli chônmunhwa chôngchaek pangan e kwan han yôn'gu* [Research on Seoul City's supply of public housing and policy suggestions regarding professional management]. *Report for Chinbo shindang sangsang yôn'guso* [New Progressive Party Imagination Research Institute]. Accessed July 22, 2013. http://seoul1.newjinbo.org/xe/file1/114371.

Lee, Kwan Ok. 2007. "NYMBY Is Jamming the Provision of Public Rental Housing in South Korea: An Inter-governmetal Policy Toolkit Based on Lessons from US Cases." Paper presented at Conference on Transformation in Housing, Urban Life, and Public Policy, Asia Pacific Network for Housing Research, Seoul, South Korea, August 30 to September 1.

Lee, MyungHwi. 2005. "*1950-60 nyôndae kye wa sagŭmyung sijang*" [Gye and unorganized financial market in 1950–1960s]. *Yôsông kyôngje yôn'gu* [Women's economic research] 2 (1): 127–50.

Lee, Namhee. 2005. "Representing the Worker: The Worker-Intellectual Alliance of the 1980s in South Korea." *Journal of Asian Studies* 64 (4): 911–37.

———. 2007. *The Making of* Minjung: *Democracy and the Politics of Representation in South Korea*. Ithaca, NY: Cornell University Press.

Lee, Sang-Kyung. 1997. *Kang Kyông-ae, munhak e sô ûi song kwa kyegŭp* [Kang Kyông-ae: gender and class in literature]. Seoul: Kôn'guk University Press.

———. 2009. *Na nûn in'gan ûro sal ko sip ta, yôngwôn han sinyôsông Na Hye-sôk* [I want to live as a human being: Na Hye-sôk, the eternal new woman]. Seoul: Han'gilsa.

Lee, So-Hee. 2002. "The Concept of Female Sexuality in Korean Popular Culture." In *Under Construction: The Gendering of Modernity, Class, and Consumption in the Republic of Korea*. Edited by L. Kendall, 141–64. Honolulu: University of Hawai'i Press.

Lee, Soo-Jung. 2011. "Education for Young North Korean Migrants: South Koreans' Ambivalent 'Others' and the Challenge of Belonging." *Review of Korean Studies* 14 (1): 89–112.

Lemke, Thomas. 2001. "The Birth of Bio-Politics: Michel Foucault's Lecture at the Collège de France on Neoliberal Governmentality." *Economy and Society* 30: 190–207.

———. 2002. "Foucault, Governmentality, and Critique." *Rethinking Marxism* 14 (3): 49–64.

Lenin, Vladimir I. 1939. *Imperialism, the Highest Stage of Capitalism: A Popular Outline*. New York: International Publisher.

Li, Tania M. 2007. *The Will to Improve: Governmentality, Development, and the Practice of Politics*. Durham, NC: Duke University Press.

Lim, Sung Eun, Nam Kyu Sang, and Dong Hun Oh. 2009. "*Changgi chônse chtaek i chubyôn chônse kagyôk e michi nûn yônghyang*" [The effect of public housing policy on neighborhood housing price by lease on a deposit base]. *Han'guk tosi haengjônghakhoe tosihaengjônghakpo* [Korean urban administration association's urban administration quarterly] 22 (2): 245–64.

LiPuma, Edward, and Benjamin Lee. 2004. *Financial Derivatives and the Globalization of Risk*. Durham, NC: Duke University Press.

Lukacs, Gabriella. 2010. *Scripted Affects, Branded Selves: Television, Subjectivity, and Capitalism in 1990s Japan*. Durham, NC: Duke University Press.

———. Forthcoming. "The Labor of Cute: Net Idols, Cute Culture, and the Social Factory in Contemporary Japan." *positions: asia critique*.

Martin, Randy. 2002. *Financialization of Daily Life*. Philadelphia, PA: Temple University Press.

Marx, Karl. 1990. *Capital*. Vol. 1. London: Penguin Books.

———. 1991. *Capital*. Vol. 3. London: Penguin Books.

Massumi, Brian. 2002. *Parables for the Virtual: Movement, Affect, Sensation*. Durham, NC: Duke University Press.

Mauss, Marcel. 1954. *The Gift*. London: Cohen and West Press.

McHugh, Kathleen, and Nancy Abelmann, eds. 2005. *South Korean Golden Age Melodrama: Gender, Genre, and National Cinema*. Detroit, MI: Wayne State University Press.

McNally, David. 2011a. *Global Slump: The Economics and Politics of Crisis and Resistance*. Oakland, CA: PM Press.

———. 2011b. "Mubarak's Folly: The Rising of Egypt's Workers." Accessed June 5, 2013. http://davidmcnally.org/?p=354.

Mies, Maria. 1986. *Patriarchy and Accumulation on a World Scale: Women in the International Division of Labour*. London: Zed Books.

Moon, Seungsook. 2002. "Carving Out Space: Civil Society and the Women's Movement in South Korea." *Journal of Asian Studies* 61 (2): 473–500.

———. 2005. *Militarized Modernity and Gendered Citizenship in South Korea*. Durham, NC: Duke University Press.

Morison, Ora. 2012. "OECD Warns of Long-Term Pain for Jobless Youth." *Globe and Mail*, economy section, July 12. Accessed June 5, 2013. http://www.theglobeandmail.com/report-on-business/economy/oecd-warns-of-long-term-pain-for-jobless-youth/article4402044/.

Muraki, Noriko. 2007. "Alternatives and Ambivalence: College Women and the Transformation of Middle-Class Citizenship in Japan's New Economy." PhD diss., University of Illinois, Urbana-Champaign.

Nam, Hwasook. 2009. "Shipyard Women and the Politics of Gender: A Case Study of the KSEC Yard in South Korea." in *Gender and Labour in Korea and Japan: Sexing Class*. Edited by Ruth Barraclough and Elyssa Faison, 78–102. London: Routledge.

National Statistics Office. 2006. *2005 In'gu chutaek ch'ongjosa: yôsông, adong, koryôngja, hwaldong cheyakcha, hon'in yôllyông, irin kagu pumun* [2005 population and housing census report: Women, children, the elderly, people with disabilities, ages of marriage, and single household]. Seoul: National Statistics Office.

———. 2009. *"Kajok"* [Family]. In *2009 t'onggye ro po nûn sôul yôsông* [Seoul women viewed through statistics in 2009]. 73–173. Seoul: National Statistics Office.

Navaro-Yashin, Yael. 2009. "Affective Spaces, Melancholic Objects: Ruination and the Production of Anthropological Knowledge." *Journal of the Royal Anthropological Institute* 15(1): 1–18.

Nelson, Laura C. 1991. "The Korean *Chonsei* System of Housing Rental." Master's thesis, University of California, Berkeley.

———. 2000. *Measured Excess: Status, Gender, and Consumer Nationalism in South Korea.* New York: Columbia University Press.

———. 2006. "South Korean Consumer Nationalism: Women, Children, Credit, and Other Perils." In *The Ambivalent Consumer: Questioning Consumption in East Asia and the West.* Edited by Sheldon M. Garon and Patricia L. Maclachlan, 188–207. Ithaca, NY: Cornell University Press.

Noritake, Ayami. 2013. "A Place of Diversity and Change: Gender, Space and Agency in a South Korean Marketplace Area." PhD diss., National Australian University.

Ogle, George E. 1990. *South Korea's Dissent within the Economic Miracle.* London: Zed.

Oh, Joong-Hwan. 2007. "Economic Incentive, Embeddedness, and Social Support: A Study of Korean-Owned Nail Salon Workers' Rotating Credit Associations." *International Migration Review* 41 (3): 623–55.

Oh Yông-chae. 2009. "*Chogûpchûng pôri ko ûimi it nûn sam*" [Meaningful life by giving up speedy, anxiety-driven life]. *Nongmin sinmun* [Farmer's newspaper], cover section, August 14. Accessed June 9, 2010. http://www.nongmin.com/article/ar_detail.htm?ar_id=165067&submenu=articletotal.

Ôn'nine. 2006. *Ôn'nine pang* [Sister's room]. Seoul: Gallion.

——— 2007. *Ôn'nine pang 2* [Sister's room 2]. Seoul: Gallion.

———2009. *Ôn'ni tûl chip ûl naga ta: Kajok p'akke sô kkumkku nûn saero un sam sûmul yôdul kaji* [Sister's left home: Twenty-eight kinds of new lives dreamed living apart from parents]. Seoul: Esse.

Paik, Young Gyung. 2011. "'Not-Quite Korean' Children in 'Almost Korean' Families: The Fear of Decreasing Population and State Multiculturalism in South Korea." In *New Millennium South Korea: Neoliberal Capitalism and Transnational Movements.* Edited by Jesook Song, 130–41. London: Routledge.

Pak Chu-yông. 2006. *Paeksu saenghwal paeksô* [Everything about a good-for-nothing]. Seoul: Minûmsa.

Pan Chông-ho. 2008. "*Chôigûn sodûkpunbae hyônhwang kwa cho'se mit kongchôkijôn ûi chaebunbae hyogwa: Kûlloja kagu rûl ch'ungsim uro*" [Recent distribution of income and redistribution effect of tax and public transfer based on workers' households]. *Nodongribyû* [Labor review] 42: 22–40.

Panitch, Leo, and Sam Gindin. 2008. "The Current Crisis: A Socialist Perspective. *The Bullet*, September 30, 142. Accessed June 5, 2013. http://www.socialist-project.ca/bullet/bullet142.html.

Park Hyejung. 2008. *Ch'ônho tong 423 pônji, kû sigan ûl palki ta* [Trace the history of 423 Ch'ônho tong]. Seoul: St. Francesco Sisters' Association, Sonya's House.

Park, Hyun Ok. 2011. "For the Rights of 'Colonial Returnees': Korean Chinese, Decolonization, and Neoliberal Democracy in South Korea." In *New Millennium South Korea: Neoliberal Capitalism and Transnational Movements.* Edited by Jesook Song, 115–29. London: Routledge.

Park, Jin-Kyung. 2008. "Corporeal Colonialism: Medicine, Reproduction, and Race in Colonial Korea." PhD diss., University of Illinois, Urbana-Champaign.

Park, Kyeyoung. 1997. *The Korean American Dream: Immigrants and Small Business in New York City.* Ithaca, NY: Cornell University Press.

Park, Kyung Tae. 2008. *Sosuja wa Han'guk sahoe* [Minorities and Korean society]. Seoul: Humanitas.

Park, Mi. 2005. "Organizing Dissent against Authoritarianism: The South Korean Student Movement in the 1980s." *Korea Journal* 45 (3): 261–89.

Park, Shinyoung. 2007. "Korean National Housing Corporation's Role and Achievements in Housing Policy." Paper presented at Conference on Transformation in Housing, Urban Life, and Public Policy, Asia Pacific Network for Housing Research, Seoul, South Korea, August 30 to September 1.

Park, Seo Young. 2012. "Stitching the Fabric of Family: Time, Work and Intimacy in Seoul's Tongdaemun Market." *Journal of Korean Studies* 17 (2): 383–406.

Park, So Jin, and Nancy Abelmann. 2004. "Class and Cosmopolitan Striving: Mother's Management of English Education in South Korea. *Anthropological Quarterly* 77 (4): 645–72.

Perelman, Michael. 2000. *The Invention of Capitalism: Classical Political Economy and the Secret History of Primitive Accumulation.* Durham, NC: Duke University.

Peritz, Ingrid. 2012. "Protest: 'Would You Consider the Total Incapacity to Make Change in a Society an Awakening? I'm Not So Sure.'" *Globe and Mail*, section F: Globe Focus, June 2, 1, 6–7.

Portes, Alejandro, Manuel Castelles, and Lauren A. Benton. 1989. *The Informal Economy: Studies in Advanced and Less Developed Countries.* Baltimore, MD: Johns Hopkins University Press.

Povinelli, Elizabeth. 2006. *The Empire of Love.* Durham, NC: Duke University Press.

PRESSian Book Editorial Board. 2008. *Uri nŭn muôt ŭl hal kôt in'ga? Minjuhwa 20 nyôn, Han'guk sahoe rŭl tola ponda* [What are we going to do? Looking back on Korean society at the twentieth anniversary of democratization]. Seoul: PRESSian Book.

Pyôn Miri, Sin Sang-yông, and Cho Kwanjong. 2008. *Seoul ŭi ilin kagu chŭngga wa tosi chôngchaek suyo yôn'gu* [Single person household and urban policy in Seoul]. Seoul: Seoul Development Institute.

Quijano, Anibal. 2000. "The Growing Significance of Reciprocity from Below: Marginality and Informality under Debate." In *Informalization: Process and Structure.* Edited by Faruk Tabak and Michaeline A. Crichlow, 133–65. Baltimore, MD: Johns Hopkins University Press.

Rah Ûi-hyông. 2005. *Kajokhyông puûi kongsik 33* [Thirty-three formulas for making wealth for the family]. Seoul: Miliôn hausû.

Read, Jason. 2001. "The Hidden Abode of Biopolitical Production: Empire and the Ontology of Production." *Rethinking Marxism* 13 (3): 24–30.

Renaud, Bertrand. 1989. "Understanding the Collateral Qualities of Housing for Financial Development: The Korean "Chonse" as Effective Response to Financial Sector Shortcomings." INU discussion paper no. 49. Washington, DC: World Bank. Accessed June 6, 2013. http://www.google.com/url?sa=t&rct=j&q=&esrc=s&frm=1&source=web&cd=6&ved=0CD4QFjAF&url=http%3A%2F%2Fwww-wds.worldbank.org%2Fservlet%2FWDSContentServer%2FWDSP%2FIB%2F2000%2F04%2F05%2F000178830_98101902155215%2FRendered%2FPDF%2Fmulti_page.pdf&ei=KbewUb_JDMaQigLgz4Go

CQ&usg=AFQjCNGjBlOZwgKqi_XPFFOzUeXKZxUQHQ&sig2=dyI59EjHu job-GVC-ZfmsQ.

Republic of Korea. 2005. "*Che 1cha chôchulsan koryônghwa sahoe kibon kyehôik 2006–2010, sero maji ha nûn haengbok han chulsan kwa nohu saeromaji pûl'laen 2010*" [The first platform of master planning to promote birth and child care, 2006–2010: "New anticipation plan" for low fertility and aging society for the years to 2010]. Accessed August 29, 2013. http://stat.mw.go.kr/front/statData/publicationView.jsp?menuId=41&nttSeq=10297&bbsSeq=7&nPage=4&searchKey=&searchWord=.

———. 2010. "*Che 2cha chôchulsan koryônghwa sahoe kibon kyehôik 2011–2015, sero maji ha nûn haengbok han chulsan kwa nohu Saeromaji pûl'laen 2015*" [The second platform of master planning to promote birth and child care, 2011–2015: "New anticipation plan" for low fertility and aging society for the years to 2015]. Accessed August 29, 2013. http://www.bokjitimes.com/downManager.do?a=WO4%2BZ%2BS5VlbpeiamVZy5PoOaougvJceK&b=Gsvtg7JimAkad4H47kQ4I Q%3D%3D&c=nBmND1hxXmw%3D&d=o0m4rIWeKpo%3D.

Roitman, Janet. 2007. "The Right to Tax: Economic Citizenship in the Chad Basin." *Citizenship Studies* 11 (2): 187–209.

Ronald, Richard, and Lynne Nakano. 2013. "Single Women and Housing Choices in Urban Japan." *Gender, Place and Culture: A Journal of Feminist Geography* 20 (4): 451–69.

Roy, Ananya. 2005. "Urban Informality: Toward an Epistemology of Planning." *Journal of the American Planning Association* 71 (2): 147–58.

———. 2011. "Slumdog Cities: Rethinking Subaltern Urbanism." *International Journal of Urban and Regional Research* 35 (2): 223–38.

Saisho Hiroshi. 2003. *Morning-Style Person* [Achi'm hyông in'gan]. Translated by Choi Hyôn-suk. Seoul: Hansû midiô.

Sang Nam-Kyu and Oh Dong-Hun. 2009. "*Changgi chônse chutaek i apatû maemae kagyôk e michi nûn yônghyang e kwan han yôn'gu*" [A study on the effect of the Shift project on the housing price]. *Pudongsanhak yôn'gu* [Journal of the Korean real estate analysts association] 2: 149–65.

Sassen, Saskia. 2000. "The Demise of Pax Americana and the Emergence of Informalization as a Systemic Trend." In *Informalization: Process and Structure.* Edited by Faruk Tabak and Michaeline A. Crichlow, 91–115. Baltimore, MD: Johns Hopkins University Press.

Sato, Barbara. 2003. *Japanese New Woman: Modernity, Media, and Women in Interwar Japan.* Durham, NC: Duke University Press.

Seo, Dong Jin. 2008a. "*Sosong ha nûn sahoe, pulp'yông ha nûn chuch'e: Chôngch'i chôk in chôhang ûl ôttôk'e chuch'ehwa hal kôt in'ga?*" [Society of disputes, subject of complaints: How can we subjectify political resistance?] In *Kwangjang ûi munhwa esô hyônsil ûi chôngch'i ro: Minjuhwa 20nyôn, minjujuûi nûn nugu ûi irûm in'ga?* [From the culture of plaza to the politics of reality: twenty years after democratization, whose name is the democracy?] *Tangbi ûi saenggak 01* [Thoughts of Tangbi 01], 132–50. Seoul: Sanch'aekcha.

———. 2008b. "*Muôk ûl hal kôk in'ga hok ûn chôngchi chôk chuchehwa ran muôk in'ga?*" [What to do, or what is political subjectification?] *Chaûm kwa moûm* [Consonant and Vowel] 1 (Fall): 314–27.

———. 2009. *Chayu ûi ûiji chagi kyebal e ûi ûiji* [The will to self-empowerment, the will to freedom]. Seoul: Tolbaege.

———. 2012. "Credit Haven: Temporal Fluctuation of Domestic Money in South Korea and Its Cultural Economy of Financialization." Paper presented at the workshop "Debt: Cultural, Moral and Political Economic Dimensions," Lancaster University, United Kingdom, July 12. Accessed October 21, 2013. http://www.crossroads2012.org/sites/www.crossroads2012.org/files/pictures/ CS%202012%20-%20Confirmed%20sessions%20and%20papers.pdf.

Shin, Hyun Bang. 2008. "Living on the Edge: Financing Post-Displacement Housing in Urban Redevelopment Project in Seoul." *Environment and Urbanization* 20 (2): 411–26.

Shin, Jiweon. 2002. "Social Construction of Idealized Images of Women in Colonial Korea: The 'New Woman' Versus 'Motherhood.'" In *Women and the Colonial Gaze*. Edited by Tamara L. Hunt and Micheline R. Lessard, 162–73. New York: New York University Press.

Shin, Kwang-Young. 2003. *Han'guk ûi kyegûp kwa pulpyôngdûng* [Class and inequality in South Korea]. Seoul: *ûlyu munhwa sa*.

Slater, David Hunter. 2003. "Class Culture: Pedagogy and Politics in a Japanese Eorking-Class High School in Tokyo." PhD diss., University of Chicago.

Smart, Alan. 2003a. "Impeded Self-Help: Toleration and the Proscription of Housing Consolidation in Hong Kong's Squatter Areas." *Habitat International* 27 (2): 205–25.

———. 2003b. "Financialization and the Role of Real Estate in Hong Kong's Regime of Accumulation." *Economic Geography* 79 (2): 153–71.

Sông Chi-hye. 2008. "*Pihon yôsông ch'ukche sô man nan si wa mal om nûn radio*" [Poetry and soundless radio encountered in Pihon women's festival]. *Yôsôngjuûi chônôl Ilda* [Feminist journal Ilda], culture section, June 9. http://www.ildaro. com/sub_read.html?uid=4452&section=sc7.

Song, Jesook. 2006a. "Family Breakdown and Invisible Homeless Women: Neoliberal Governance During the Asian Debt Crisis in South Korea, 1997–2001." *Positions: East Asia Cultures Critique* 14 (1): 37–65.

———. 2006b. "Historicization of Homeless Spaces: The Seoul Train Station Square and the House of Freedom." *Anthropological Quarterly* 79 (2): 193–223.

———. 2007. "'Venture Companies,' 'Flexible Labor,' and the 'New Intellectual': The Neoliberal Construction of Underemployed Youth in South Korea." *Journal of Youth Studies* 10 (3): 331–52.

———. 2009a. "Between Flexible Life and Flexible Labor: The Inadvertent Convergence of Socialism and Neoliberalism in South Korea." *Critique of Anthropology* 19 (2): 139–59.

———. 2009b. *South Koreans in the Debt Crisis: The Creation of Neoliberal Welfare Society*. Durham, NC: Duke University Press.

———. 2010. "'A Room of One's Own': The Meaning of Spatial Autonomy for Unmarried Women in Neoliberal South Korea." *Gender, Place and Culture: A Journal of Feminist Geography* 17 (2): 131–49.

———. 2011. "Situating Homelessness in the Post-Developmental Welfare State: The Case of South Korea." *Urban Geography* 32 (7): 972–88.

————. Forthcoming. "Gendered Care Work as 'Free Labor' in State Employment: School Social Workers in the Education Welfare (Investment) Priority Project in South Korea." *positions: asia critique*.

————, and Yoonhee Lee. forthcoming. "Educating Mothers through Media: Deviancy of Children and Therapy Market/Culture." In *Mothering in the Age of Neoliberalism*. Edited by Melinda Vanderbeld Giles. Toronto: Demeter Press.

Sotiris, Panagiotis. 2012. "Greece: From Despair to Resistance." *The Bullet*, February 14. http://www.socialistproject.ca/bullet/598.php.

Spivak, Gayatri C. 1999. *A Critique of Postcolonial Reason: Toward a History of the Vanishing Present*. Cambridge, MA: Harvard University Press.

Stack, Carol B. 1974. *All Our Kin: Strategies for Survival in a Black Community*. New York: Harper & Row.

Stacy, Judith. 1987. "Sexism by a Subtler Name? Post-industrial Conditions and Postfeminist consciousness in the Silicon Valley." *Socialist Review* 17 (6): 7–28.

Standing, Guy. 2011. *The Precariat: The New Dangerous Class*. London: Bloomsbury Publishing.

Stewart, Kathleen. 2007. *Ordinary affects*. Durham, NC: Duke University Press.

Sunder Rajan, Kaushik. 2006. *Biocapital: The Constitution of Postgenomic Life*. Durham, NC: Duke University Press.

Tabak, Faruk. 2000. "The Rise and Demise of Pax Americana and the Changing Geography and Structure of Production." In *Informalization: Process and Structure*. Edited by Faruk Tabak and Michaeline A. Crichlow, 71–90. Baltimore, MD: Johns Hopkins University Press.

Tangdaebipyông. 2008. "*Kwangjang ûi munhwa esô hyônsil ûi chôngch'i ro: Minjuhwa 20nyôn, minjujuûi nûn nugu ûi irûm in'ga?*" [From the culture of plaza to the politics of reality: twenty years after democratization, whose name is the democracy?]. In *Tangbi ûi saenggak 01* [Thoughts of Tangbi 01]. Seoul: Sanch'aekcha.

————. 2009. "*Kûdae nûn wae ch'otpul ûl kkûsyôtna yo? P'ongnyôk kwa ch'ubang ûi sidae, cho'tppul ûi minjujuûi rûl tasi munnûn ta*" [Why did you turn off the candlelight? The era of violence and expel and reconsidering democracy of candlelight]. *Tangbi ûi saenggak 02* [Thoughts of Tangbi 02]. Seoul: Sanch'aekcha.

Tangherlini, Timothy R. 1998. "Shamans, Students, and the State." In *Nationalism and the Construction of Korean Identity*. Edited by Hyung Il Pai and Timothy R. Tangherlini, 126–47. Berkeley: Institute of East Asian Studies, University of California.

Tsujimoto, Toshiko. Forthcoming. "Negotiating Gender Dynamics in Heteronormativity: Extramarital Intimacy among Migrant Filipino Workers in South Korea." *Gender, Place and Culture: A Journal of Feminist Geography*.

"Troubled Tigers: Asia Needs a New Engine of Growth." January 31, 2009. *The Economist*, 75–77. Briefing. Asian Economies. Accessed October 19, 2013. http://www.economist.com/node/13022067.

U Sôk-hun. 2009. *Hyôngmyông ûn irôtke choyonghi* [Revolution comes this quietly]. Seoul: Redian.

———— and Pak Kwôn-il. 2007. 88 *manwôn sedae: chôlmang ûi sidae e ssû nûn hûimang ûi kyôngjehak* [Generation of 880 dollars: economics of hope written in the era of despair]. Seoul: Redian.

Virno, Paolo. 2004. *A Grammar of the Multitude*. Los Angeles: Semiotext(E).

Vogel, Erica. 2011. "Converting Dreams: Money, Religion and Belonging among Peruvian Migrant Laborers in South Korea." PhD diss., University of California, Irvine.

Vosko, Leah F. 2000. *Temporary Work: The Gendered Rise of a Precarious Employment Relationship*. Toronto: University of Toronto Press.

Wacquant, Loïc J. D. 1999. Inside "The Zone." In *The Weight of the World: Social Suffering in Contemporary Society*. Edited by Pierre Bourdieu et al. Translated by Priscilla Parkhurst Ferguson, 140–67. Stanford, CA: Stanford University Press.

Wagele, Elizabeth. 1997. *The Enneagram of Parenting: The 9 Types of Children and How to Raise Them Successfully*. New York: HarperCollins.

Wagele, Elizabeth. 2001. *Eniôgraem ûiro po nûn uri ai sokmaûm: sôngkyôk e matsun sônggong chôk in chanyô yangyukpôb* [The Enneagram of parenting: The nine types of children and how to raise them successfully]. Translated by Kim Hyôn-chông. Seoul: Yôn'gyông media.

Wagenknecht, Sahra. 2012. "The Euro Crisis and the European Fiscal Pack." *The Bullet*. Translated by Samuel Putinja. June 29. http://www.socialistproject.ca/bullet/663.php.

Ward, Kathryn, ed. 1990. *Women Workers and Global Restructuring*. Ithaca, NY: ILR Press, Cornell University.

Ward, Kevin. 2006. " 'Policies in Motion,' Urban Management and State Restructuring: The Trans-Local Expansion of Business Improvement Districts." *International Journal of Urban and Regional Research* 30 (1): 54–75.

Winson, Anthony and Belinda Leach. 2002. *Contingent Work and Disrupted Lives: Labour and Community in the New Rural Economy*. Toronto: University of Toronto Press.

Woo-Cumings, Meredith, ed. 1999. *The Developmental State*. Ithaca, NY: Cornell University Press.

Woolf, Virginia. 1929. *A Room of One's Own*. London: Hogarth Press.

Yakabuski, Konrad. 2012. "Age Collides with Politics in Today's Fractured Quebec." *Globe and Mail*. August 4. Accessed June 6, 2013. http://www.theglobeandmail.com/news/national/age-collides-with-politics-in-todays-fractured-quebec/article4462141/?page=all.

Yang, Mayfair. 1994. *Gift, Favors, and Banquets: The Art of Social Relationship in China*. Ithaca, NY: Cornell University Press.

Yang, Sunyoung. 2010. "Internet Addicts as a New Form of Industrial Reserve Army in a Computer-Mediated Society." Paper presented at the Historical Materialism Conference, York University, Toronto, May 13–16.

Yea, Salie. 2005. "Labor of Love: Filipina Entertainer's Narratives of Romance and Relationships with the GIs in US Military Camp Towns in Korea." *Women's Studies International Forum* 28 (6): 456–72.

Yi Chong-sô. 2009. "*Ch'ukche ka toen ch'umo*, kû u'ul han panbok: Roh Moo Hyun ûl kiôk hamyo" [Memorial that became festival: In memory of Roh Moo Hyun]. *PRESSian*, political section, May 30. Accessed June 9, 2009. http://pressian. com/article/article.asp?article_num=60090529083122&section=01.

Yi Hye-rin. 2007. "*30 tae singgûl yôsông k'aeriktô, TV sûkûrin 'ôn'ni' ka ttûnda'*" [Single women in their thirties, soaring stars as TV drama characters]. *Segye ilbo*, culture section, January 15, 12.

Yi Nam-chu. 2008. "*Ch'otpul hangjaeng ûl nôm ô chônjin haja*" [Let's move on from the Candlelight Vigil demonstration]. *Kyegan changbi* [Creation and critique quarterly] 141.

Yi Tae-hûi. 1999. "*Ajôssi ka anieyo, tonieyo: 15 sal ûi wonjokyoje ch'unggyôk*" [He is not elder, but money: shocking teen prostitution]. *Han'gyôre sinmun*, social section, November 18, 19.

———. 2008. "*Ch'otpul ûi chigujôn*" [Global struggle of Candlelight Vigil]. *Han'gyôre 21* (719). Accessed June 22, 2013. http://legacy.h21.hani.co.kr/ section-021003000/2008/07/021003000200807140719005.html.

Yi Tae-yông. 2009. "*Ch'otpul 1nyôn p't kwa kûrimja*" [Light and shadow of Candlelight Vigil anniversary]. *Segye Ilbo*, May 3. Accessed June 8, 2010. http://shinchun. segye.com/Articles/Issue/Leading/Article.asp?aid=20090503001938&subctg1= 02&subctg2=.

Yi Yu-jin. 2007. "'*Chagi man ûi pang' e 'yôsông ûi mom' irûkyô seuda*" ["Women's body" was commemorated in the "Room of One's Own"]. *Han'gyôre Newspaper*, February 27. Accessed July 22, 2013. http://www.hani.co.kr/arti/society/women/193235.html.

Yô Kôn-chông. 2008. "*Chônchejuûi ûi yuhok*" [Temptation of totalitarianism]. *Kyegan Pipyông* [Critique quarterly] 20 (Fall): 4–10.

Yu Mi-ri. 1998. "*Kajok sinema*" [Family cinema]. Seoul: Koryôwôn.

Yun Sang-don. October 14, 2005. "*Yôsông chônyong apatû imdae hamni ta*" [Women's public housing has begun]. *Seoul sinmun*. Accessed June 8, 2010. http://www. seoul.co.kr/news/newsView.php?code=seoul&id=20051014011008&keyword= %BF%A9%BC%BA%C0%FC%BF%EB%C0%D3%B4%EB.

Zaloom, Caitlin. 2004. "The Productive Life of Risk." *Cultural Anthropology* 19 (3): 365–91.

Zhang, Xia. Forthcoming. "One Life for Sale: Youth Culture, Labor Politics, and New Idealism in China." *positions: asia critique*.

Žižek, Slavoj. 2000. *The Fragile Absolute: or, Why Is the Christian Legacy Worth Fighting for?* London: Verso.

Audiovisual Materials (Listed by Translated Title)

Battlefield of Cash (*Jjôn ûi chônjaeng*). 2007. Directed by Tae-u Chang. Produced by Yông-sôp Kim. Seoul: Seoul Broadcast System.

It Is Fine for a Woman to Be Single (*Sing'gûl ira to kwaench'an a*). August 18, 2007. Directed by Yu Hyôn. Written by Han Suk-cha. Produced by P. Choi. Sponsored by Munhwa Broadcasting Company (MBC).

Slumdog Millionaire. 2008. Directed by D. Boyle and L. Tandan. Produced by C. Christian. United Kingdom: Celador Films, Warner Brothers.

Song of Acclamation for Farmers: Project of Returning to Farming (*Nongbiôch'ôn'ga: kûinong pûrojektû*). June 19, 2009–November 25, 2011. Seoul: Seoul Broadcasting System.

Truth or Dare of Multiple Fortunes Association, a Rotation Credit among Gangnam Elites (*"Kangnam kûijok kye, tabokhoe ûi chinsil keim"*). November 27, 2008. Episode no. 694 of *Kû kôt i algo sip tta* [That I would like to know]. Directed by Choi Sam-ho. Seoul: Seoul Broadcast System.

Young Hope Thrown out to the Street: Youth Homeless Is Increasing (*"Kil ûi e pôryôjin chôlmûn hûimang: ch'ôngnyôn nosukcha ka nûl ko itta"*). July 26, 2008. Episode no. 678 of *Kû kôt i algo sip tta* [That I would like to know]. Directed by Im Ch'an-muk. Seoul: Seoul Broadcasting System.

Index

A *Room of One's Own*: 1929 essay
of Virginia Woolf, 17; theatre
productions of, 15, 17–18, 21
affect: in comic books, 84, 89;
conflicting channels of, 15–16,
80, 82, 88; definition of, 3, 64;
of enjoyment, 76–78, 87; labor
of, 99n17, 113n14; public sphere
changes in, 85–86, 91, 94; of social
mourning or social duty, 79–81, 88;
understanding neoliberal subjectivity
through, 64–65, 83
after-school education. *See* education,
private
aging society, 1, 10, 89, 104n8. *See also*
fertility, low
Asian Financial Crisis, 1–2, 7; arrival
of global finance through, 13, 20,
55, 59; crisis of masculinity during,
73; in history of Korean capitalism,
60; on homelessness, 22, 77, 105n14;
popularity of monthly rent during,
47; state neoliberal policies during,
69, 111n8

bank loans, 3, 12; discriminatory
policies, 44, 94, 104n8; for
households, 42–43, 45, 48, 103n4;
priority for corporations, 42,
47–48, 50, 55; for unmarried
people 8, 43–44. *See also* housing
loans
Battlefield of Cash, 106n25
Berlant, Laurent: on cruel optimism,
113n12; on lateral agency, 5, 81–82,
87
big corporations. *See* conglomerates
(*chaebôl*)
Busan, 5, 11; international film festival
of, 21, 101n15

Candlelight Vigil Mass Demonstration,
86, 91–92, 113n18, 114n19
capital: finance capital or financial
capital, 13, 40–41, 55, 59–60,
110n48; productive capital or
industrial capital, 59–60. *See also*
capitalism; money capital
capitalism, 63, 65, 73, 83, 95; classic
case in the west, 12, 41, 60,
100n32; globalizing or neoliberal, 4,
7, 40; Korean developmental, 13,
41, 55, 59, 60, 80. *See also* global
financialization

for housing, 34–36. *See also* single women: parental regulation of

sexual safety, 33, 34–35. *See also* sexual moral regime

Shift, 45, 110n49

single women: cosmopolitan or abroad experience of, 25, 26, 46, 64, 70–72; households by, 5–6, 13, 23, 34; media representation of, 6, 8, 33, 71–72, 77; parental regulation of, 2, 18–19, 25–30, 70; surveillance of sexuality, 19, 34, 45, 103n; statistics of, 5–6; within women's movement, 89–90. See also *mihon yôsông; pihon yôsong; sexual moral regime; toksin yôsông*

social employment, 88

social enterprises, 88

social mobility, 47, 105n19; disinterest in, 73; through maneuvering *chônse*, 53; of women, 108n37

social mourning, 79, 80; labor of, 15, 81–82, 86100n34; affective regime of social duty, 5, 79, 88, 89

social networks, 13, 23, 94; as alternative to family, 31–32; informal markets' reliance on, 41, 43; rotating credit associations through, 51–52; of student activists, 33; of women, 68, 72

speculation, 12, 13, 41, 59; distinctions between U.S. and Korea, 55, 60

state welfare, 45, 58, 69, 77, 105nn14–15

state-planned economy, 42, 55, 106n24. *See also* developmental state

student activism: cultural changes in, 85; dogmatic codes of, 67–68, 72; as generational experience, 5, 93, 98n10; in human rights movements, 14, 18, 32–33, 113n; legacy of, 15, 21, 77–78, 86–87; discrimination against women in, 4, 33, 66, 76; National Liberation, 67–68; of rank-and-file (*see* rank-and-file activists). *See also* leftist movements

subalterns, 82, 93, 100n31; movements of, 3; and money capital, 13; propaganda music for, 83, 86, 92, 112n4

surplus population, 7, 65. *See also* youth un(der)employment

technologies of the self: 4, 14, 65, 74, 83, 98n11, 110n2. *See also* self-management

tenants, 3, 46, 53–54, 98n8

toenjang nyô (soybean women), 72

toksin yôsông (never-married women), 21. *See also* single women

travel, 15, 66; as alternative to emigration, 46, 105n17; cosmopolitanism through, 19, 21, 101n10; through foreign media, 72; freedom of, 20, 70; leisure of, 31, 67–68, 86, 87

TV dramas and films: cultural liberalization in, 20–21, 71; domestic works about unmarried women, 71–73; in relation to comic books, 83–84, 89

urban life, 10, 11; high price of, 18, 39, 47, 49, 71; leaving countryside to pursue, 23–29, 39, 47; retreat from, 102n24; speed of industrialization in, 73

usury, 43, 50, 59, 60, 108n38; TV show about 106n25. *See also* informal loans; rotating credit associations

Virno, Paolo, 7

Wacquant, Loic, 81–82

women's labor, 7–8, 90. *See also* care work; caring; irregular work

women's movements, 4, 14, 18, 21, 101n16, 113n16; and removal of *hojuje*, 9; in Seoul, 68–69; and single women's issues, 89–90; and state partnerships, 76

women's organizations, 30, 43, 69, 70, 86, 88; community network in, 58, 90. *See also* women's movements